Deep Darkness

Ed Gilkey

authorHOUSE®

AuthorHouse™
1663 Liberty Drive
Bloomington, IN 47403
www.authorhouse.com
Phone: 1-800-839-8640

First published by AuthorHouse 11/13/2009

ISBN: 978-1-4490-4563-0 (sc)

Printed in the United States of America
Bloomington, Indiana

This book is printed on acid-free paper.

Chapter 1

Shark Feeding Frenzy! - the headlines screamed. *Thousands of sharks sighted from Cape Hatteras to Virginia Beach!*

Tim dully pondered his good fortune at having selected Myrtle Beach, South Carolina, for their honeymoon.

Absently he thumbed through the newspaper to the sports page.

Red Sox continue their slide, fourth loss in a row.

Hmmmm....., she wouldn't want to hear that.....it might spoil their so far, perfect honeymoon.

Honeymoon-whoever came up with that expression sure had Shawnee Trace in mind. He thought back to how every guy on the beach since they got there had made it a point to check her out. And who could blame them. Tall, auburn haired with those beautiful green eyes, and *"she don't think she's beautiful"*- the words to that country song ran through his head again as he gazed at her sleeping.

He could scarcely believe that a flat tire on his old pickup truck had prompted her to stop and help in that rainstorm.

There she stood, under her meager umbrella-that barely covered her-offering to shield him from the summer storm that had him scrambling. She was so striking-in her yellow windbreaker and her white cut-off shorts, and she was so –what was the word-

SWEET-that he couldn't believe his eyes. She probably got more soaked that he did that day back in June.

He looked over his shoulder at her sleeping form-Wow! -she's All mine!-her perfect body-now bronzed by the summer sun.

Mrs. Timothy McGregor-Mrs.Shawnee Trace Overton McGregor.

Shawnee-what a strange yet different name for such a strange and different girl. Her smile, her eyes, her laugh, her little girl innocence about so much. Here they were husband and wife on their honeymoon. Another 3 days of experiencing all that each of them were and looking at life as the great fun it can be. Tim again gazed at her sleeping-I am so lucky-she's so perfect.

She had been driving to see her parent's gravesites on that day in June-though she hardly looked like a mourner in her cut-offs and bare feet, driving that old VW bug.

She had accepted his invitation to meet for coffee later that same night and both of them were, well, smitten.

They were together as often as they could be throughout the rest of the summer. She was staying in Covesville with her maiden aunt and Tim raced through his workday to see her each night.

He thought about their fast paced romance...Their simple pleasures-hiking up Crabtree Falls, trips to Big Meadows, swimming in the <u>Shenandoah</u>...

He couldn't help but recall their inadvertent swim the day in late July when they took his small johnboat out on the Shenandoah and suddenly, she hooked that catfish. Tim's dog-Grayboy, was so excited that he jumped in after the fish before she could even land it. Grayboy's plunge had caused them to flip and they ended up in each other's arms laughing then kissing. Tim couldn't resist and he proposed right there in the middle of the river. Grayboy swam to shore, the catfish was last seen pulling her rod and reel toward Winchester and Tim had a fiancé'.

Tim thought about today's schedule-their plans were very unplanned-she was that way-somewhat haphazard-always spontaneous--just fun to be with. Fun to be married to. He

2

thought-'*I should go back to bed-it's only 6:15*'.Back home he'd have been up and at work for over 2 hours .

Suddenly the phone rang.

Who could possibly be calling?-nobody knew where they were – this had to be a wrong number.

Tim raced to the bedside- hoping that the phone would not awaken Shawnee. Too late-she had reached over and answered before he could intercept the call. She handed him the phone and rolled over.

"Yes-I see-well how did you find us- oh-of course-Yes- As soon as possible – Yes Ma'am-thank you-Good-bye

"Princess-that was Ingrid, they need me to return right away."

"Timmy-lets pretend the phone didn't ring-this is our honeymoon,"she yawned.

"How did they find us- this was our secret place"- she said pulling him to her.

"Ingrid said that Rolf knew where we were-that I told him...."

"Timmy, let's just say that we thought they said come tomorrow."

"Trace, I can't-we need to leave today, as soon as possible"

"Ok, my newly married husband" she purred, "but not just yet."

At 9:45, showered, fed and hurriedly packed, they slid toward each other from either side of Tim's 4X4. The 1967 short bed Chevy had little indoor storage space and since it looked like rain-they packed everything in the cab. Cozy,but then she loved cuddling with Tim. They nestled together for the long drive back to Virginia.

"By the way- the Sox lost last night – 4 to 2. Manny and Papi homered but Timlin couldn't save it"- Tim offered as they headed out onto the highway. "Blown save, blown honeymoon,-well guess what Mr. Timothy Paul McGregor?- I love you anyway! You are my favorite memory of all!"

Chapter 2

"Funny you should say that"- Tim offered.

"Say what?"

" You're my favorite memory of all- I didn't know that you were a country music fan."

"I'm not, not really anyway. Why, whose lyrics did I use this time?"

"Merle Haggard."

"Merle Haggard- let's see, Okie from Muskogee, Fightin' Side of Me..."

"So , you are a closet music fan after all," Tim teased.

"Well not really, but I am a patriot and those are 2 songs that my teacher made sure we heard when I was in high school."

"High school? What class?"

"US History. Mr. Yeklig was a child of the 1960's and he showed us how American culture split over the war."

"War?"

"Vietnam," she continued. "He said that he had been a hippie but had changed-actually God had changed him . He told us that some of his generation never came home-some left for Canada, while some like the Clintons blamed America for everything. Strange, a man like Bill Clinton who hated our own military, eventually got to order it around. He was just so amoral!!

"Whoa", intoned Tim. "You just crossed two lines we said we weren't going to cross – religion and politics- so let's get back to something like..."

"Us?" she cooed.

"Us !" he grinned. Have I told you are my everything today? I love you."

They kissed and momentarily the pickup veered out of its lane.

"Tim, what can be so all fired important that a big company like ERWACHE needs my one and only husband back from his honeymoon? Don't they employ thousands of able-bodied people? Why you? Why now?"

"Well maybe not thousands of workers," Tim corrected." More like hundreds, but the vast majority are not able bodied."

"I've seen some of the workers and they look like they are able bodied to me! Of course, your body is"...she nibbled on his ear... the old truck veered again.

" Now stop or I may have to pull over for the night", he pled unconvincingly.

"Could we?" she begged.

"I'll make it up to you- I promise- now that we are married we can go on lots of romantic getaways-like Afton Mountain in the fog or the Tangier Island cruise..."

"Just as long as we don't leave Virginia- isn't that what ERWACHE 's policy is?"

"Yep, I had to get special permission to go to leave the state"..

"To test out that able body?" she played.

"Yes," he smiled, " to test out my able body and to get to know the sweetest girl in the whole world."

The truck slowed down considerably and a blast from a passing big rig finally got Tim to concentrate on the road.

"Really Timmy. Why not some one else, why does it have to be you?"

"Those hundreds of workers who seem normal?" he led off.

She nodded.

"Almost all of them are either deaf, dumb or both."

"Really? How do they find those people? Why would you hire...?"

"The handicapped? The Krauses have a working arrangement with the State of Virginia- they hire the deaf and dumb and provide housing as well."

"But where can they find so many?"

"There's a connection with the Woodrow Wilson Rehabilitation Center in Fishersville. That's sort of where they found me."

"But you both speak and hear, why were you..."

"There?"

"Yes , there."

" I was kind of an exception after my parents were killed . I didn't... couldn't speak for about 2 years," his voice just trailed off.

"Oh, Timmy, I'm sorry," she squeezed his hand and then lifted it to kiss it. "I know it's painful."

They were quiet for a few moments and then she turned her attention on the radio.

"Do you mind?" she asked.

"Not at all, but I don't think my presets will work down here. Just see what you can find."

The first song brought a smile to their faces.

"Well I love her but I love to fish...
right now I'm on this lakeshore,
sitting in the sun,
yeah, I'm sure it will hit me
when I walk through that door tonight,
Yeah, I'm gonna miss her,
Looky there, I've got a bite.

"That was the Fishing Song by Brad Paisley," intoned the female dj in a thick drawl.

"Could that be our song?" he teased.

"Not on your life Mr. McGregor!" she giggled.

The country songfest continued.

She liked *Have you Forgotten* (about the 9/11 attacks) but struggled with Hank Jr.'s *Family Tradition*.

"May I?" she asked looking at Tim cautiously as she toyed with the radio knob.

"Of course," he said absently as he peered in the rear view mirror at the van that seemed to be their traveling companion.

"Try that one," he suggested as the strains of *Bad Company* filled the cab. His air guitar impression and the lyrics caused a slight frown to grow on her face.

"Now see here McGregor, you are *not* Bad Company! Not my husband!!!!" She poked him so hard in the ribs and he was laughing so hard , that they barely kept 2 wheels on the pavement.

As he fought to keep the truck under control, she spun the dial again, just in time to hear :

Well there's Victory in the Lord I say,
Victory in the Lord!
Cling to the Father and Praise His Holy Name, and
Don't go A-Ridin on that Long Black Train...

"Amen," she added quickly without hesitation. "Alan Jackson?"

"Josh Turner," Tim corrected. "See I told you that country music is where it's at! And speaking of Alan Jackson," they both listened quietly as the station played *Where Were You When The World Stopped Turning*(another tribute to 9/11/01).

They were both reflective after that until Shawnee broke the silence by asking, "Where were you , Tim?"

"I was waist deep in the Shenandoah, watching my best spinning reel and my favorite rod heading North, my dog paddling frantically for shore and holding my future wife !"

The truck's speedometer slowed to under 40 as they embraced again.

As before, a passing car got Tim to focus on driving once more.

That radio station faded and she tried her hand again at finding some satisfactory music.

Suddenly she lurched forward, listening intently.

A nasally voice protested, "But Mr. Whitaker, that would mean I'm 180 degrees out of phase!"

A second male voice- "Translation?"

First voice- "I have erred grievously!"

The voice of an exasperated teenage girl, " You mean you're wrong Eugene?"

"It's Odyssey!!" Shawnee squeaked.

Tim looking up- "I don't see any..."

"On the radio, Adventures in Odyssey!"

"Adventures in Odyssey?"

"Tim, just listen for a few minutes ,ok?"

He nodded.

They did. She laughed lightly at the 12 minutes of banter and he found himself discovering another phase of her personality. Here was this beautiful woman, his wife. So perfect in every way and yet so much like a child in her trusting and straight forward manner. She seemed so much like a little girl-so open , so honest so .. what was the word .. so ...

"So what'd ya think?"

"About?"

"About Odyssey?'

The show *had* been entertaining, written for kids but with enough punch to keep adults listening. He wasn't displeased- just confused as the show signed off.

"Focus on the Family?"

"Oh, yes! I grew up listening to Odyssey. It's a radio series with Christian lessons for families. My folks and I used to try not to miss it. It was carried by the local Bible Broadcasting Network station and my folks and I loved listening .As an MK (Missionary Kid) we didn't have a lot of social activities but we sure enjoyed Odyssey. My mom was real good at guessing how the stories might turn out and I can still hear my daddy chuckling..." her voice faded as she teared up.

"Still hurts huh? " Tim volunteered.

"It's ok," she said pulling herself together. "I know I'll see them again and talking about them does me good."

"You sure?" Tim asked as he slid his arm around her shoulder and pulled her close, sharing a long hug.

She nodded.

"So ..."

"So my mom and dad, Lucille and Kenneth Overton were called to the mission field years before I was born. They served in Uganda, Malaysia and Fiji before being called to witness to tribes here in our own country. They were here in Oklahoma working among the Native Americans when I came along. My mom loved the Shawnee people in particular and the rest is as they say – is history"- she said stretching.

"Called?" Tim quizzed.

"Missionaries and pastors, at least in the Christian faith, believe that God has made a special call to them-not just anybody can spread the good news about Jesus Christ in foreign lands where the water is polluted, there are no toilets and no one has heard of bug spray. It takes special people to do that and my mom and dad were special."

"Hmmm..." Tim contributed.

"Let me rephrase something I just said. We can all witness for Jesus but not everyone does or wants to or goes overseas."

Tim perceived that they were headed into that gray area again- religion- so he attempted to steer the conversation into another direction. "Were you angry when they died? I know I was when my parents were killed ."

"For a long time I couldn't understand why God took them home, especially since they were hit by a drunk driver. But His plan is not our plan and His ways are not our ways. They were walking back from a Bible study on the reservation and were killed almost instantly-at least, that's what the sheriff said. I woke up the next morning and I was an orphan. I was 12."

"And then you moved to Virginia?   "

"I was taken in by another missionary family and eventually moved back here to the Missionary Learning Center in Rockville. I lived at the center and went to Patrick Henry High School in Ashland. In my senior year, my great aunt, Maria Ludlov, contacted me. I didn't even know that I had a great aunt but she insisted that I come to visit her in Covesville, so I did."

"So what's the story behind that creepy old house?"

"It wasn't always creepy. Aunt Mae wasn't always old either. The house has just gone down since she has gotten elderly."

"So you moved here when you were 20?"

"19 ½", she corrected. "I tried community college for 1 ½ semesters when she called me and asked if I could come to look out for her."

" That's my girl. Always looking out for others, whether it's holding an umbrella in the rain for a hillbilly with an old truck or helping a distant relative – you are so special!" he hugged her.

" It's just the way I was raised." Treat others as you like to be treated- the Golden Rule. You have heard of the Golden Rule haven't you Timmy?"

"The way I heard it – He who has the Gold makes the rules, isn't that it?" He winced as she poked him in the ribs.

"That's awful."

"That's the way it seems anyway..."

"Ok , enough about Shawnee Trace. Wanna talk about your folks?"

Tim shrugged.

"I think it helps to keep their memories alive. How about if I tell you about your parents?"

Tim looked at her as if she had 3 heads.

Finally, Tim said – "Ok, let's see how good your memory is."

She started. " You are the only child of Jim and Cindy McGregor. You were born prematurely and weighed only 3 pounds when you were born. You all lived in Luray and your dad was a butcher."

" Butcher? Where did that come from?" he demanded.

"Opps, sorry- he was a chef ?" she guessed.

"You're O for 2. Want to try 1 last time ?"

"He was a fireman and ..."

"Strike 3. He and mom owned a small grocery . He was also commissioner for the Valley League."

"And the Valley League is ?"

"Each summer, college kids from all over head to the Shenandoah Valley to play baseball. I used to go all over with Dad to see the games."

"That's why you know so much about the valley!"

" Not just the valley but what's under the valley."Tim asserted.

"Growing up around the caverns, he and mom started spelunking as hobby. They..." (he could tell by the quizzled look on her face that he had to explain spelunking)

were cavers. We used to go exploring where few had traveled before. There are lots of caves in this part of Virginia . One day when I was 10, we were just about to climb out of one... just another 200 feet or so to get to the surface, when the roof collapsed. I was in front of them- they always made sure that I followed them in and led them out- safety first..."

"The Golden Rule" – she challenged, "always think of others first."

"How the Krauses ever got me to work underground again I'll never know-but I guess I don't think about it much anymore. I just do it," he finished as again his voiced faded.

"OK, McGregor," she affirmed . "New topic. Let's talk about our house ! OUR house. Doesn't that just sound dreamy?"

"Dreamy? That must be a married term. I never thought much about my place being dreamy."

"But it's ours Timmy. Just the 2 of us" –she nestled closer to him.

"Well, technically the company owns the house. It's been fine for me and Grayboy and I'm sure he won't mind sharing it with you," he kidded. "It'll be a tight squeeze but ' *We Can Make It If We Try*', he sang in his worst falsetto.

"All 6 of us?"

"6?"

"Six. I want 2 boys and 2 girls!" she declared.

They had had this conversation before. Tim was not fond of children and she loved them, so this was one of their "twilight zone" subjects. He would listen but not really hear.

Hoping to dodge the kid issue, Tim began, "I think we could start redecorating this week, after work... My old bachelor pad just won't be the same. How could it be, with my love there with me?"

She hugged him closely and the Chevy wobbled noticeably.

"How much will the company allow us to do? Can we add on?"

The "house" in question had been Tim's home since he was 18. It was a strange building, not much bigger than a decent sized tool shed. The place was made out of local stones- one floor, a large room that served as living, sleeping and cooking, and a small bathroom with shower. Perhaps it's one saving grace was the large stone fireplace at the far end of the room. She had absolutely loved it the first time she saw it but knew it could never accommodate more than 2 people.

"That's all up to Ingrid. Ingrid and Dr. Jo are real demanding but they probably won't mind a few changes."

"They don't strike me as being very friendly. You've been with them what, 8 years?"

"Ten," he corrected.

"So you don't think they will be too much in favor any changes?"

"Like I said, a few, but they are very reserved and don't like too much change."

"Maybe I'm wrong but I think they don't like me already. They were so distant or cold or..."

"They are just real proper. And besides, I don't care if they don't like you. I LOVE YOU and that's all that matters."

She kissed him on his neck then nibbled on his ear. Tim fought to keep the truck on the road.

"Still-didn't you think them strange at the wedding? Here they have known you for 10 years, raised you for part of that time and they seemed like they couldn't get out of there fast enough."

Their wedding had been at the Covesville Presbyterian Church, partially in deference to Aunt Mae. It was easier for her to attend since she was now wheel chair bound. The exterior of the old church was somewhat dreary that rainy day but its sanctuary was quite welcoming. Shawnee was radiant in her white gown while Tim was quite uneasy in his only suit.

7 people had attended the service: the pastor, the church organist, the Krauses, Aunt Mae, Tim and Shawnee. The ceremony lasted 10 minutes and the only reception had been punch and a small cake at Aunt Mae's. The pastor and the organist had briefly attended out of courtesy but the Krauses virtually fled.

Shawnee had not voiced it but she detected disgust on the part of the Krauses as she introduced them to Aunt Mae. Ingrid Krause, in particular, was very reluctant to shake hands with Aunt Mae.

"I just wish I felt better about them," she sighed.

They had to stop twice for gas as the old truck was very thirsty. In truth, the truck was Tim's 2nd love beyond Grayboy. All that would be changing with his wife now in 1st place, dog second and truck third. It was a 1967 Chevy ½ ton 4X4 short bed pickup, now immaculately redone. Tim had spent most of his pre-Shawnee, non-fishing time, working on the Chevy.

She liked the way that Tim had restored the truck and how it sat high above the interstate. "This boy has real potential," she had told herself early in their courtship. "If he can do this with an old truck, maybe they could restore Aunt Mae's home and maybe they could eventually raise a family there and", her mind was racing as Tim eased the beast into the Virginia twilight.

It was getting darker earlier now with summer on the wane and it was difficult to make out the Blue Ridge range as they churned up Interstate 64 toward Charlottesville.

"Well, we aren't alone", Tim motioned skyward.

"Huh?"

Tim pointed toward the dirigible passing parallel to the Interstate. "It's one of ours."

Chapter 3

"Zion Crossroads-can we please stop Tim, I need to use the restroom."

"Again?" he teased.

"Well you know how we pregnant ladies are" she mocked as he recoiled in horror.

"Ok, here we are" he announced as the truck shuddered to a halt."This will give me a chance to call in and see if I need to pick up anything in Charlottesville."

He studied her as she walked toward the restroom. He wasn't alone. Every guy in the parking lot watched her sway by. She was so sweet and so easy to look at.

"She don't know she's beautiful" he whistled again to himself as he reached for the pay phone.

He had not yet made his call when she walked up and slid into his arms, squashing the hopes and dreams of many a nearby trucker.

Tim had dialed the main number only to be put on hold. He was kissing his wife deeply when a growl emanated from the other end of the phone.

"McGregor, you're at Zion Cross Roads by now aren't you?" It was Rolf, ERWACHE's foreman.

"Yes, but how..."

"Just a guess-based on your travel time and when you were called-get here quickly," he snarled abruptly hanging up.

Tim gingerly hung up the phone and looked into those beautiful green eyes. Shrugging his shoulders, he said, "Well come on my now wife-let's head home."

"Now wife? "

"Yep, in the old days, Virginia wives didn't live every long due to disease and problems at child birth, so they were always introduced as your "now wife."

"Planning on bumping me off heh McGregor?"

"Not a chance," he said picking her up, smothering her with a kiss and then whisking her into the truck. The truckers looked on in awe.

They settled down for the last leg of the trip and the truck's supercharger roared to life.

"Timmy, how did Rolf know where we were?"

"He said he guessed."

"Oh, I thought the Graf Zeppelin spotted us."

"If it spotted anything, it spotted the most beautiful girl in the world"...the Chevy again headed toward the shoulder of the interstate...

Chapter 4

The dirigible loomed large in the growing darkness.

The "Graf Zeppelin" that Shawnee had alluded to was not *the* Graf Zeppelin of history. It was a modern adaptation of the lighter- than- air ships that had once been the pride of Germany between the World Wars. History's tragic zeppelin, *Hindenburg*, had exploded in 1937 in that terrible disaster at Lakehurst, New Jersey, thus pretty much ending public interest in balloon flight.

The Graf Zeppelin or dirigible was now synonymous in Central Virginia with ERWACHE, and probably gaining in notoriety each year on the Goodyear blimp. The main difference was that Goodyear used it's blimp as a public attraction whereas the ERWACHE fleet was purely business.

The ERWACHE dirigibles were famous along the Route 64 corridor between Charlottesville and Virginia Beach. They now however, were mostly nocturnal since the blimps that Dr.Jo commissioned had created monstrous traffic snarls in the early days as motorists often watched the great craft rather than the highway.

The use of the huge ships had proven to be an incredible innovation in moving massive quantities of materiel from one place to another. By using the plentiful non-explosive gas helium, Dr. Krause had been experimenting with TODTs

(Topographically Oriented Delivery Transports) 3 of which were under slung each of the massive 800 foot long ships.

Each TODT (which was nothing more than a supersized cargo container) could carry tons of raw coal or tons of supplies for disaster relief.

ERWACHE and its balloon fleet had been used to bring relief to victims of Hurricane Katrina and various floods. The giant craft were not bound by washed out roads or ruined railroad trestles.

The dirigibles could fly in all but the worst weather since the TODTs provided tremendous stability and ballast even when empty.

Dr. Krause and his wife had been lauded many times by the United States government and were frequent visitors to the Clinton White House.

Although he never spoke of it, Dr. Krause had been a research scientist at the University of Virginia, until his department was disbanded in the 1970's. It was alleged, that someone in his department had absconded with $ 4 million in grant money but no charges were ever brought and the money seemed to have vanished. Dr. Jo had returned to his native Prussia, shortly thereafter marrying Ingrid Stoss, a striking blond with flashing blue eyes. Although she was many years his junior, the couple lit up any room. With almost white blond hair, one might have thought them albinos, but they were far from that.

Ingrid was now in her 40's but could easily pass for late 20's, while Dr. Jo was probably in his late 50's but he did not look much past 35. In Tim's estimation they both looked the same as they had 10 years ago when he joined them.

The Krauses were very exacting and precise people. They monitored their caloric intake, and then chronicled the amount of sleep and exercise that they got each day. Tim had often thought, 'If being that precise has made them look that good for so long, maybe there's something to their routine.'

ERWACHE was set up as a model of Prussian efficiency- at least Tim had heard someone once describe it as such. Every aspect of the corporation had been minutely planned. Even though Tim had lived in Lovingston for the past 10 years, and had been "raised" by the Krauses, there were still segments of the ERWACHE organization that he had seen only on the scale model that Dr. Jo kept in his office.

ERWACHE seemed to have revitalized Lovingston when the Krauses founded it there in the 1970's. The town, like many in the rural Virginia mountains, had prospered until the coal seams played out in the 1950's. Nelson County used Lovingston as the county seat but nowadays there was precious little growth that wasn't in some way tied to ERWACHE. Lovingston was pressed hard against the mountains to the east and Route 29 to the west. The latter rose up and slid down mountains and valleys leading north to Washington, D.C. and south to Roanoke, Virginia. The road was 2 lanes in each direction dissected by massive clumps of foliage in some parts and very little in other places. Largely it remained somewhat a relic of earlier days. Both sides of the highway going in either direction bore the remains of generations of families that had worked the land for its crops and worked under the earth for the coal that had once fueled American industry. In essence, Route 29 was locked in time when the Krauses arrived.

Dr.Jo realized that a severely depressed economy might allow him great leeway and power. He was correct on both accounts. When he purchased much of Lovingston, he was given virtual free reign in certain aspects of community life. Before long, the handicapped workers were indeed housed and hired by ERWACHE but at a price. A sociologist studying the town would find it to be much closer to a "company town" of the 1870's than a hive of free enterprise in the 1980's.

Town center had the court house, 3 lawyer's offices, a tractor repair place and notably 4 churches, 3 now closed. True there were a few stores but old town Lovingston continued to have a listless look.

ERWACHE was another matter altogether.

When viewed from the air, the whole operation could best be described in relation to the face of a huge clock. Almost every hour of the clock's face had a corporate function tied together by a tram line.

Everyone was to board the small train only at the 1 o'clock position. All workers, Tim included, were to board the tram line between 4:30 and 5:30 am, Monday through Friday. This was a somewhat inconvenient arrangement since almost all workers lived in the town and the town was at the 5 o'clock position. Some mornings there was congestion getting into the parking lot which sat adjacent to the 1 o'clock entrance, but Tim like most others, had grown used to following Dr.Jo's directives.

Between 1 and 5 on the clock, the Krauses had built their castle; at least, Tim considered it a castle. Their estate was actually protected on sides, north and south, by mountains, with a scenic large lake to the east and the distant Route 29 to the west.

The mountains north of "Castle Krause" were pristine and would probably remain so. The mountains to the south (at about 2:30 on the clock face) were being slowly developed into a hill climb course so that Dr.Jo could try out his stable of racing cars. Ingrid's passion, downhill skiing, was being addressed as at least 3 slopes were under construction, slopes that she hoped would attract young skiers to the area.

Looking down on the ERWACHE schematic, occupying the 5 o'clock position was Lobo's Den. No structure in the town more closely hugged the mountains. This was another of Ingrid's pet projects- the rehabilitation of an antique shop into a 'place to go' in Lovingston. Its dual goal seemed to be to attract traffic from Route 29.

The "Den" had an Espresso bar filled with all the lattes and trendy exotic blends Mrs. Krause could stock. Next to the Espresso bar, was a small area for reading the 15-20 newspapers that were delivered daily. 4 or 5 tables were set up expressly for the playing of chess. There were 8-10 bookcases filled with books, some for sale, and all for loan to any of the locals. Her favorite accomplishment was the stage that she had had built where local musicians could entertain on Tuesday, Friday, or Saturday night. No alcohol was served until 7 pm on Saturday nights and then only until 10 pm. The menu included health food and German beer, for those rare individuals who liked both. Locals seldom attended Lobo's Den, since there were cheaper, less restrictive watering holes in Charlottesville.

Upstairs at the 'Den' was a large open area that Ingrid was using as an antique loft, but she wanted something else, something that would attract young people. Perhaps an art gallery or trendy apparel shop- she wasn't quite sure.

One of the unique features of the 'Den' was that it had direct access to the tramline that connected all parts of the ERWACHE structure. By way of the rear exit, you entered a tunnel equipped with a slight escalator that met the tramline on the east side of the mountain. Tim had often wondered why the employees had to travel so far to gain access to the tram and not just proceed through Lobo's Den, but that was one of Ingrid's rules and she controlled access.

At the 6:30 position on the ERWACHE clock, and east of the mountains, was the company's infirmary. The Krauses had built an absolute state of the art facility which was operated 24/7 by stern, though well schooled, European doctors. There was always at least a skeleton crew ready to address any injury since much of the Krause empire entailed many hazardous jobs. Health care was free to all employees and yearly physicals were mandatory.

Moving via tram from the infirmary toward the 12 o'clock position, things got real busy, especially in the 8 to 10 o'clock region.

On the surface, at approximately 8, were the hog pens and a processing plant. Swine were brought in by rail as the Krause property on the east bordered the CSX's north-south rail line. This plant was staffed almost entirely by the hearing and speaking impaired. Inside the hog processing plant, Prussian efficiency was again on display, as the Krause's insisted on hospital like cleanliness. Scientists on loan from foreign universities were constantly conducting tests on the animals.

To feed the animals, Dr. Jo had planted 80 acres of corn, just inside the tramline and east of the lake that Ingrid had insisted on. Stocked with bass and ready to be fished by any invited visitor, the lake had a small flotilla of boats. Self-sufficiency seemed to be one of ERWACHE's goals.

Below the hog works were literally miles of coal seams newly developed by ERWACHE. It was these seams that were the main source of income for the corporation. Dr. Krause had made international connections with nations like China and India, who were buying tons of Virginia coal in a time when most Americans had never even seen coal. ERWACHE coal it could be argued, was contributing mightily to the daily haze that emanated from both nations. However, since Dr.Jo had been very persuasive with the Clinton-Gore team in 1992 and again in 1996, they had made sure that the Kyoto Treaty would not affect his business. In the final draft, the world's two most populous nations and heaviest users of coal, were not to be restricted and ERWACHE made a fortune.

Prospects looked favorable for large amounts of Virginia coal to end up in Asia for years to come.

The coal was loaded into the TODTs, which were then connected to the respective bellies of ERWACHE's fleet of zeppelins. The zeppelin port, sometimes referred to as the LP (launch/landing pad) was at the 11 o'clock position on the clock dial.

The majestic looking craft could only be described in one word-HUGE. Each of the 3-vessel fleet was 800 feet long and 150 feet high. Control of the massive ship was accomplished in the command gondola, which was a 20 by 40 foot cabin in the bottom center of the blimps. When the TODTs were connected, each of the great ships was over 250 feet in height.

ERWACHE engineers had been experimenting with alcohol and methane to power the massive Daimler engines each blimp had. If ethanol from cornfields or methane from the pigs could be harvested, then yet another area of ERWACHE could be self-sufficient.

12 o'clock on the clock face was reserved for Dr.Jo's true obsession, his automobile restoration shop. It rivaled any such facility in the world. Porsche, Maserati, and exotic Formula 1 racecars were meticulously restored in on section while

American classics like Cord and Duessenberg sat in another area. Even the more mundane Model A and Jaguar had his interest. There were constant inquiries from car collectors around the world but seldom did Dr. Jo open his shop to visitors. Occasionally, TODTs returning from Virginia Beach contained nothing but antique cars to be refurbished.

Within the bowels of this massive shop, there was an area for zeppelin issues, a machine shop capable of metal fabrication and a general repair shop for ERWACHE vehicles-tram included. It was probably watching these technicians that had interested Tim in both restoration and mechanics.

Adjacent to the landing area were the great helium storage tanks that enabled the ships to rise. There was a fire station next to the storage facility but it was manned only during the week and during daylight hours. There being little concern about fire since helium is not explosive, the station was there should any other element of the operation need help.

Chapter 5

It was to this quaint company town that Tim was bringing his new bride. At almost 11:30 pm, the Chevy came to rest in front of Tim's house, which would soon be *their* house.

Grayboy barked mightily from the fenced in back yard and Tim smiled at Shawnee as she descended from the truck.

"Home, my lady," Tim said as he took her hand.

"Our Home," she cooed and they embraced.

Grayboy continued from the gate and Tim weakly tried to silence him- "SHHHHHHH!" Tim couldn't see that the dog was no longer barking a welcome but a challenge to the same white van that had slowly trailed them home. The van sat out of Tim's sight but in close proximity to the house.

Mr. and Mrs. McGregor grabbed their few pieces of luggage and headed toward the front door.

"Before you say anything, close your eyes"... he whisked her up in his arms and carried her over the threshold.

Inside was a brand new brass double bed which looked so inviting after their long trip.

"Oh, Timmy! You are so romantic! Let's try it out!" she giggled.

"In a minute, let me let Grayboy in or we won't get any sleep tonight."

"I wasn't thinking about sleeping, not just yet anyway," she smiled.

Grayboy came in, greeted them for a few minutes then headed for his bed over by the fireplace. She excused herself while Tim switched on the small air conditioner that cooled the entire house. He had just checked his answering machine when he looked up to behold his bride in her newest negligee.

Laughing together, they flew into the new bed.

R I I I I I I I I I I I I I I I I I I I I N G G G G G   !
RIIIIIIIIIIIIIINNNNGGGGGGG!

"Who could be???"

"Hello?" Tim fairly snarled. He gazed at the clock face- it read 11:50.

"Tonight? Can't it wait? 45 minutes? Yes sir, I'll be right there. Should I..."

He looked into those beautiful green eyes and shook his head. "I can't believe this, why me? Why now? I'm sorry princess that was Dr. Krause himself."

"Timmy you know I'm a keeper," she said as she helped him find his shoes. "I'll keep the bed warm for you," she smiled. "Just be careful and hurry home," she said as she snuggled up close to him and kissed him deeply.

"A night meeting," he continued in disbelief. "We never have meetings- why a night meeting"- Tim muttered as he headed toward the door.

Grayboy, you keep my lady safe, ok?"

Grayboy tilted his head, walked over and lay down next to the new bed.

She stroked his head and said "Don't worry about us-we'll be fine." Tim turned off the light as he headed out.

45 minutes later, the few department heads and Tim met with Dr. Krause in the conference room over the zeppelin shop.

The owner and architect of ERWACHE, Dr. Josef M. Krause spoke excitedly but concisely, as was his style. Foreign affairs were going to radically transform ERWACHE and soon.

"The government has given the go ahead to the use of more coal. The Arabs have pushed petroleum costs to the point that ERWACHE along with several rival companies have the opportunity to move a lot of coal soon. We are uniquely positioned to really corner the market. No one has achieved what we have achieved. We will go down in history as the greatest producer of coal. This will mean almost nightly flights to Norfolk and we will have to turn up production."

He turned to face Tim squarely. "You will be in charge of all routing of the coal from the seams to the surface while Ernst will supervise the loading into the TODTs. This, by the way, Tim, is a promotion and a wedding present." Dr.Jo's expression did not change-no sign of humor or gentility-just a matter of fact statement.

Tin winched, he did not like being the center of attention if even for a moment. His tired mind could barely comprehend what had just happened and he might have summoned up a question but...

Dr. Jo abruptly said, "Now everyone is dismissed. Be here sharply at 4:30 for more instructions."

Chapter 6

Tim awoke the next morning to the delightful yet unexpected smell of fried apples.

He peered wearily at the clock and it reported 3: 54.

He slowly sat up and gazed at the form of his new bride busily preparing their first breakfast. She had been asleep when he returned at 1:39 am but Grayboy had met him at the door, confirming that all was well

He got out of bed and hurriedly dressed. Slowly he approached Shawnee who was humming softly to herself. He slid his arms around her and she quickly responded by turning and kissing him.

In between kisses he managed, "Why are you up?"

She gently whispered," Because Grayboy and I figured that if we didn't get up with you this morning that we would miss you altogether".

Tim's puzzled look led her to explain.

"Grayboy wanted to go out about 3. I checked your alarm and we decided that whatever that meeting was about last night, would take you away from us for the day. So he stood watch while I cooked. We figured that we could sleep later today while 'daddy' was away".

They laughed and kissed more deeply only to be stopped by Grayboy whining.

"Whoa, look at the time. I've got to run. What will you 2 do today?" he asked as he grabbed the bag lunch she had prepared.

She handed him her early morning creation and his look of uncertainty made her smile." It's edible -it's an old family recipe- fried apples wrapped in soft pancakes and seasoned with just the right amount of buttered grits"

Tim laughed out loud- "Trace- I wish I could stay and "...he clung to her.

"I know, I know, I love you Timmy. Now don t worry we will be fine. We will go visit Aunt Mae. I may even let Grayboy drive. We'll be here waiting for you at 5:15"

His heart was heavy- he really wanted to stay in bed with his bride – wasn't this still really their honeymoon? Where was the justice in all this? Sure the promotion sounded great and –The Promotion! He hadn't even remembered to tell her.

The pickup slid sideways into the parking lot at 4: 24. Just enough time to catch the tram.

He plopped down next to a weathered looking older man- probably a hog processor Tim guessed. His cordial "Good morning" was met with a blank stare. Great! Tim thought a non-talker. Or was he non -hearing? It was too early to think about anything.

He sunk down for a quick snooze. Before he nodded, he thought of her and remembered he had not told her he loved her- I will make it up to her tonight.

Shawnee and Grayboy did sleep for a short time after Tim left but both were up and about by 8.

She surveyed their home.

"Grayboy, we both love Daddy but we are going to have to redecorate. This is décor is definitely from his early bachelor period. Maybe we can go shopping this weekend and show Mr. McGregor how a home is supposed to look," she mused.

Grayboy seemed interested and approached her with his favorite tennis ball in mouth. He seemed to sense that she was staying and since she was, well, why not play ball.

Tim's dog was part Labrador and part Golden Retriever but had a gray coat, thus the name.

She looked into those deep brown eyes and thought how human they appeared- so accepting. They played ball in the back yard for about 15 minutes and then she said, "Ok, you win, let's go for a ride and see Aunt Mae. Come on, bring your ball."

At first, the big dog appeared unsure of what she expected. Her creaky old Volkswagen was a far cry from the seat he was accustomed to in the pickup.

They made their way out onto Route 29 North toward Covesville. Her beetle struggled with the hill and the railroad crossing, one of those few in Virginia that had no crossing gate or warning light.

At last having made the hill, they drove into the yard of Aunt Mae's very run down estate. The house was a 2-story frame that had been white and quite pretty in its day.

She thought about her high school history class as she gazed at the house. They had studied World War I and the American poet, Joyce Kilmer who was killed in France. Her teacher Mr. Yeklig, had had them read Kilmer's *The House with Nobody in It*. Every time she thought about this house, she was saddened because soon Aunt Mae would pass and the once proud house would probably be the house in the poem.

Aunt Mae wasn't really Shawnee's aunt. Her uncle Mike Jeffries had fought in World War II and had met Maria Ludlov somewhere in Europe in the spring of 1945. From the account that had passed down through the family, she had found him, wounded, hiding from the Gestapo, and had shielded him from the Nazis. He recovered and they fell in love. He brought her home to Ivy, Virginia, and they had planned a large wedding for late 1946.

They were fixing up the Covesville estate when he caught pneumonia and died. Maria was so distraught and lost that she never married. The family resolved that she should receive his life insurance payments and she settled down to a life of relative obscurity —working seasonally as long as she could at the Covesville apple processing plant and attending the small church. She had few friends and over the years much of Mike's family had forgotten about his *"war bride"*. It was not until a very distant relative from Chicago, doing a family tree search, had made the connection, that Shawnee even knew about her "aunt".

Since Shawnee's wedding, arrangements had been made with social services to have a caregiver with Aunt Mae except through the night. The elderly woman was able to do some things for herself but the UVA medical center had suggested that she would probably never walk again and that speech would be difficult at best.

Shawnee let herself into the great entrance hall and moved toward the parlor where Aunt Mae had been staying since mid –July.

Mae looked more frail than Shawnee had remembered her to be. She awoke with a start at the appearance of Grayboy, who had dutifully followed Shawnee in.

"Good morning Aunt Mae. I hope we didn't frighten you. This is Grayboy, Tim's- our dog."

The dog licked the withered hand of Aunt Mae and a glimmer of a smile crossed her twisted lips.

Throughout the next 2 hours, Shawnee carried on what proved to be a mostly one-sided conversation, relating the saga of the last almost 2 weeks. The lady who was to care for Mae, Helen, a large black woman, arrived about 9 but Shawnee had urged her to relax for a while so that Aunt Mae could be updated.

At nearly 11, Shawnee could see her Aunt tiring. She called for Helen and together they washed, and changed Mae and saw to it that she ate some before she napped.

"Miss Overton, I been prayin for your Aunt. She surely is a fine lady."

"Thank you, but," she said –flashing her wedding and engagement rings, "remember its Mrs. McGregor now and anyway Shawnee is what I prefer. Thank you for caring for Mae."

Helen nodded.

"You know it's strange, I've only known her for about 1 ½ years but it seems I've always known her. I feel so sorry for her. She's gone down so fast..."

"Yes ma'am, she seems to be slipping away from us. None of us knows how much time we have. This is the day that the Lord has made..." she began.

..."let us rejoice and be glad in it"-Shawnee finished.

They smiled at each other.

"I've been reading her the Bible and that seems to comfort her and she sleeps better. One night 'fore I went home, she kept making signs 'bout this book-"she handed Shawnee a thin faded blue book with no title.

Shawnee opened it and peered at the photograph of a young handsome man in army uniform-she guessed to have been from the WWII era. Under one arm was a wooden crutch that bore much of his weight as his left leg was heavily bandaged.

Hung on his right arm, smiling slightly, was a beautiful blond girl –Shawnee guessed to have been about 18. What struck her the most about the photo was how thin the girl was.

"Uncle Mike and Aunt Mae?" she guessed.

"'Deed I don't know "offered Helen.

Thumbing through the pages, Shawnee found no more pictures but a handwriting that she could not read. It wasn't that the writing was so poor, it was actually quite beautiful – it was just written in what she guessed to be Russian or German.

"Could this be my aunt's story-here all along? "We'll have to get it translated. Thank you, Helen."

"Yes ma'am. I'll be here 'til 3 then Kristina comes in until 9."

Shawnee remember Kristina well. She was from Samoa and a devout Christian. It was at Kristina's urging that Shawnee dared go on her now abbreviated honeymoon. Her aunt would be well taken care of and indeed, she had been.

"Ok, well it looks like things inside are in good shape- I think I'll mow the front lawn while Mae's asleep. I'll look in on her later."

With that, Shawnee and Grayboy headed outside. Her first stop was to put the journal into her car and to get Grayboy some water. As she entered the shed, she slipped out of her skirt and blouse and emerged in cut-offs and halter-top. She had chosen the heat of the day, though late August was less intense than July, to mow and to get some sun. She wanted always to look her best for Tim.

Meanwhile not that many miles away but hundreds of feet below the earth's surface Tim's auger came to sudden halt.

Chapter 7

Tim never minded the whistle ending the day and he couldn't wait to get home to Shawnee. Still he was required to report all abnormal incidents and this would be one of them. He kept rolling over in his mind, more pay, more prestige, I'm married now-these thoughts versus I sure miss the sunlight and my wife....

Each night the miners would join the "porkers", mechanics and other "hired help" to make the journey to Lot 1. Everyone had to be gone by 5:45 or be docked a day's pay.

Tim never lost pay in the 5 years he had been underground-but twice equipment breakdowns had caused his actions to be reviewed. Both times he was found in compliance with company policy and now even though he was tired and wanted her badly, he still had to briefly investigate what had shut him down.

This night, Auger # 12 in shaft 16, had cut through a wall into an abandoned shaft and a small cave —in had occurred. Tim, unhurt, but miffed about this impediment in his homeward trek, gazed wearily through the dust toward the hole between the now joined tunnels. His helmet lamp, revealed a rounded shape which upon further inspection proved to be a Volkswagen Beetle, face down in about 2 feet of water,

Hmm- it doesn't seem to damaged he pondered. He remembered in the early days that Dr. Jo had been recycling cars and maybe this one was one that the company had just pushed aside until later.

Darn-look at the time- I'll really have to hustle to catch the tram. With one last glance over his shoulder, he could now make out the forms of 2 other cars but had neither the time nor interest to investigate tonight. They've kept this long, another day won't matter.

Tim missed the last tram by 2 minutes but knew he could hike the distance to the balloon port and still be ok. There was the usual delay as the crews switched and the blimps had to be righted sometimes at great risk if the wind was whipping. He hopped on the tram and waited with everyone else as the balloon crew of six entered. There were the few voices on the tram as most everyone else was either deaf or dumb or both.

Wonder what kind of day it had been, at least it looked dry. He missed the sunshine and could not wait to get home.

Shawnee true to her word, at 5:15, stood at the door waiting for him. She and Grayboy had hustled home from Covesville, straightened the bedspread, and turned the air conditioner on.

She put Grayboy outback, heated up her tuna and macaroni casserole and showered. She donned her Red Sox jersey and little else.

She met him at the door and led him to the bed.

I've been dreaming about you all day," she offered.

"Me too," he muttered between kisses.

They didn't talk much mostly held each other when he sniffed- "Do you smell something bur"...

"My casserole!"- she shrieked...jumping up and turning off the now overheated burner. Their small home filled with smoke.

He laughed silently until she noticed, and then she broke into a mock sob. They both laughed and hopped back into bed. In a matter of minutes, all was forgotten, forgiven, and Tim held her close.

She began to tell him about her day when she was interrupted by his snoring. "My poor Timmy", she thought, "16 hours without rest on top off our 'lost honeymoon'"- she didn't fret she knew he was just worn out probably just 8 hours sleep out of the last 48- she concentrated on cleaning up "dinner" and offered it to Grayboy. He gingerly took it and buried it. She smiled- "what a memorable homecoming!"

At 8:20, Tim rallied and apologized for falling asleep.

"You know what Mrs. McGregor; it bothered me all day- I forgot to tell you I loved you this morning."

"You still haven't "-she teased... He took her in his arms and they kissed for a long time.

"Listen, I made myself a promise that I'd make it up to you "....

"You already have"...

"But we still haven't eaten-if we hurry we can make it to Colleen."

"Ice cream for dinner?" she protested.

He knew she loved the ice cream at the Colleen Drive in- it was a mild amusement along what was mostly a drab stretch on 29 South. She had told him that she hadn't often had ice cream as a child, MK's didn't always live like other Americans even when on furlough here in the USA. She had proclaimed Colleen's ice cream to be the best she had ever tasted.

"Ok, but on one condition. I drive."

"In your bug? We'll never make it much less make it in Time."

"It's OUR bug now and no not in the VW."

"You, driving the truck? Well I don't know..."

"Come on, McGregor where's your faith? Bet I can get us there by closing time".

Not without a little anxiety, he entrusted his keys to her and slid beside her to help officiate. He really need not have worried. When he restored the truck, he gave it all the upgrades he could muster.

She got them southbound on 29 and then punched it. The truck's massive 454 engine launched them quickly to 70.

"Whoa Susie," he protested.

"Susie? And just who is Susie? "

"It's just a figure of ..."

"What's this boost gauge for?" she interrupted.

"That's for the turbocharger but.."

"Hold on," she cautioned as the little truck screamed onward. He looked on in amazement as the figure of his wife, that beautiful figure of his wife, was now pushing them toward 140 mph.

Just as suddenly, she backed off- "That was fun!"

Tim's color was returning to his face. "Who did I marry, Shirley Muldowney"? he posed.

"Shirley who? First it's Susie then its Shirley, the name is **Shawnee**!" she laughed.

"Shirley Muldowney was a famous drag racer who…"

"I don't care about her, we're here! Let's eat".

He wondered all the way home —who is this marvelous, wonderful, mysterious girl I've married?

Chapter 8

The next month and half flew by as they settled into married life and Tim's work schedule.

She thought that ERWACHE was too demanding until she saw his paychecks. Still it seemed to her that the hours were really unreasonable, 12-14 hours a day 5 days a week. She spent much of her time with Aunt Mae, but it was obvious that Helen and Kristina were taking good care of her. Aunt Mae had made no progress in walking and spoke very few discernable words.

One rainy Saturday evening, in early October, as Tim and Shawnee sat putting together a 1001 piece picture puzzle of a rural scene, she asked:

"Timmy, can we go away for the weekend?" Grayboy and I took a ride toward Vesuvius yesterday and the leaves are so pretty. I really like fall in Virginia. I'm sorry that you can't see it. It doesn't seem fair that you are underground during the day and miss so much- it's like you work the night shift isn't it?"

Tim shook his head- "Hold on princess, let's check the calendar and see what's planned..Now where's the calendar?"

"You mean the one that had the girls on it that couldn't find their clothes before their pictures got taken? "

Tim winced- "Yes, that one".

"Well, we voted and since you weren't here, we decided that that the only girl you should be thinking of should be me and Grayboy took it and buried it."

He hugged her and laughed, "Along with the tuna and macaroni casseroles?"

She poked him in the ribs.

"I guess we'll have to rely on the company calendar"- he retrieved it from the shelf over the stove.

"There's no weekend anytime soon, let's see, we do have some time at Thanksgiving and 2 days at the end of the year. We could have gone back in September."

"But I didn't think of it back in September, "she protested mildly.

"Well, we do have October 29th off but that's not on a weekend, we could..."

"Go on a mini-honeymoon?" she offered.

"Yes, we could. Where do you want to go?'

"Just away-with you. Grayboy will be fine here. Can I pick the place?

"Of course. Just remember that I'd have to leave after work and we'd have to be back so I could make-work on the 30th. And of course, we can't leave Virginia without..."

"Approval", she finished.

"Company policy"- he stated.

"I know, I know- besides, there wouldn't be enough time to go far anyway. It's settled then, let's shake on it".

"I prefer to kiss on it," he said taking her in his arms." You know, if you would give up taking Aunt Mae to church on Sundays, we could do some weekends more often. I mean how much does she get out of the services anyway?"

"Timmy, I just couldn't do that to her. She used to love to go to the church when I first moved down here- they said she hadn't missed a Sunday in 52 years. She made it to church sometimes before the pastor did. They said one time that the train was stalled, blocking her path to church, and she either climbed over or through it to get there. It's one of the few things she seems to find comfort in."

"Why can't Helen or Kristen take her?"

"First of all, let's remember that I like to go as well. I wish a certain someone saw the need as much as he does to work on his project car on Sundays"...

The project car she alluded to was a 1932 Chevy Coupe that Tim had purchased before he met Shawnee. It was kind of a cast –off from the ERWACHE restoration shop that Tim had picked up cheaply and had hoped to restore to original condition. Unbeknownst to Shawnee, he had wanted her to have it and was hoping to give it to her for her birthday in February.

"Secondly Tim McGregor, you need to come to church," she scolded.

"Look, I promise I'll go with you some time- it's just not something I want to talk about".

It wasn't an official fight. No punches, verbal or emotional were thrown, but it was obvious to Shawnee that she had intruded into his "space".

"Ok, "she said. "I guess I'll see if Helen or Kristen can maybe take Aunt Mae some Sunday."

"That's my girl" he kissed her. "That way we might be able to leave on a Friday late and get back late Sunday."

"Well let's get the laundry together and run up to the plaza." She figured a nice non-issue like doing the laundry would smooth things over for now.

Their tiny abode was much too small to have a washer or drier and weekly trips to the Laundromat usually had been a Saturday morning affair. Today's rain, however had kept them cuddled in bed until almost noon.

The closest Laundromat was at the "plaza", actually a small strip mall, just west of 29 somewhat south of the old part of town.. They took her car and were just getting out of it when she said, "What would you say if I got a job-at least part-time. They need help here at the Food Lion and even the Antique shop in Covesville is hiring."

Tim pondered her question but also noticed that all the men within a 3-mile radius seemed to be starring at his wife. She was just a vision of beauty and it never failed, guys fawned all over her whenever they went out. His thoughts were interrupted by her jab to the arm.

"Timmy, do you see that man in the green pick-up? He's the one that came on to me the last time I tried doing the clothes during the week. He followed me, so I went to Covesville to Aunt Mae's, that way, if I had trouble, Helen or Kristen could call for help.

As Tim turned to see the man, the green truck sped away. He didn't tell her but it had Washington, D.C., plates.

Chapter 9

He couldn't stand the thought of someone coming on to his wife. Tim didn't have much, but he loved Shawnee. She always seemed so trusting, so naïve, He told himself 'I can't have her fending for herself while I'm hundreds of feet below the earth.' He decided to ask Ingrid if Shawnee could work for ERWACHE in some capacity. If that could be worked out, Shawnee could work and still be secure from creeps at the Laundromat.

He would go through the proper channels and ask to meet with Ingrid one evening after work, perhaps at the Lobo's Den.

Ingrid Krause was not unapproachable especially for someone that had been, in Tim's words, "rescued", from the Woodrow Wilson institution.

He had never thought of her a surrogate mother, she was much too business - like, almost cold.. She seemed always about her husband's work, though Tim caught up with her on the following Tuesday evening.

"Ingrid, I need to ask you a favor", Tim began slowly.
The striking blonde, put down her newspaper. "Yes?"
"Well, it's about my wife..."
"Oh, yes ", she interrupted," is she treating you well? Are you having problems already? You know, Dr.Jo and I had such grand hopes for you. Does she satisfy you?"

Tim swallowed hard, what kind of questions are these he thought.

"She's fine and we're fine," he stumbled, "it's just that I'd like her to have a part-time job. She is very concerned about her aunt and..."

"That wretched thing that was in the wheelchair at your wedding?"

"Yes, her aunt probably will not recover and a job might help keep her mind occupied, so I thought maybe ERWACHE might have some position she could fill?"

"Tim, I must be frank with you. What qualifications does she have?"

"Well, she's honest and a very hard worker. She always looks out for me and her aunt. I don't know if she can type or has any office training but I'm sure she..."

"I see. Well, send her around tomorrow at 10:00 am and I will talk to her. Send her here".

"Yes, ma'am. Thank you". He wanted to say more but knew that Ingrid had nothing left to say and probably wouldn't be listening anyway.

Shawnee did not know what to expect when she arrived at the Lobo's Den shortly before 10 the next morning. Her only real contact with Ingrid had been at the wedding, but Tim assured her that Ingrid would be approachable.

Opening the door to the Lobo's Den, Shawnee was greeted by the pungent aroma of some form of exotic coffee brewing. She was not prepared for the warm greeting she received from Ingrid.

Ingrid came forward and hugged Shawnee as if they were long lost relatives.

"My dear girl let me look at you. What a beautiful figure. You are so lovely. Our Tim did himself proud. Please sit and have some coffee."

With that, Ingrid began an hour and one half discussion of ERWACHE' s past, present and future plans. She stopped from time to time to study Shawnee. She asked very few questions about Shawnee or Tim but seemed to enjoy watching Shawnee's features.

At the conclusion of their talk, Ingrid said, "Yes, you will do nicely. I want you to work here with me, at the Lobo's Den. You have great eye appeal. We want to attract a certain clientele and I feel certain that your looks will help us do that. You will of course need to take the company physical which we can arrange today. We pay weekly; you will be needed Tuesday, Friday and Saturday nights. We open at 4 and close at 10 each night so you will still have some time with Tim. We pay $ 12.50 to start. Is this acceptable?"

"Well, this is all so sudden, I feel somewhat light headed, I... "

"Perhaps you had too much strudel. Come we will get you checked out at the infirmary."

With that, the two women exited through rear door of the Lobo's Den and boarded the side-ways escalator through the mountain to the tramline on the other side.

A special shuttle carried them to the infirmary where Shawnee was left in the care of a Dr. Hesse, a woman with pale blue eyes and a cold demeanor.

Later that night, as they undressed for bed, Shawnee described to Tim the whole day's events.

"EYE CANDY!" Ingrid might as well have called me that. "She gives me the creeps!"

"Well, Trace, you *are* beautiful."

"I don't mind you telling me that but she seemed to be looking me over the whole time like I was a piece of meat" –she protested. "I'm not some Hooter's girl,"

"You could be. Only you'd be the Queen of them all"-he teased, grabbing her around the waist and kissing her.

"Timmy, I'm your wife. She wants me to 'attract a certain clientele'. What does that mean?"

"Ingrid doesn't play. She obviously thinks you can help the business or she wouldn't have offered the job to you. What did you tell her?"

"I told her yes, although I really should have prayed about it first..."

"What's to pray about- you got a job, the pay was...?

"$12.50 to start'"

$ 12.50? Wow, that's good!"

"To do what? To stand around and look enticing? Oh, and that physical! Who are those goons in the infirmary?"

"Goons?" Tim asked quickly.

"Goons. The woman who examined me was rude and she touched me in places that ..."

"Sweetie-, all physicals tend to be a little unsettling and I remember one time when...

"That's just it Timmy. I don't remember all of it. They did the tests and gave me some shots and I must have passed out."

"Do you faint at the sight of blood or are you just allergic to needles?"

"Tim, I'm, serious. I remember wearing one of those hospital gowns when the exam began but I don't remember anything after the shots except there was the large man dressing me. I was totally embarrassed."

"Come here. I don't like the idea of anyone touching you but me either, but it's just part of the process .I'm sure everything was done within company policy".

"Maybe, but I still don't like the idea of this job-why couldn't I sell antiques in Covesville? That would be plenty safe and I'd be close to Aunt Mae as well."

"Shawnee, your aunt isn't going to be around forever. We need to think about the future."

"I know, but she's so pitiful, and she used to be so attractive. Now she's so ..."

"Wretched?"

"Tim McGregor, that's an awful thing to say!"

"I'm sorry. Those aren't my words."

"Then just whose words are they?" she demanded.

He knew he couldn't lie and he began to mentally review what Ingrid had said. Her words had bothered him too but he just wrote them off to her nature.

"Ingrid's".

"See, I told you she's creepy-she didn't like my aunt on our wedding day and I think she's going to use me at the Lobo's Den. I don't like any of it."

Tim turned off the light and reached for her in the darkness.

"Come here, my sweet. Let me calm your fears."

Two hours later, with Tim fast asleep, she got up and turned the reading light on over their one chair. She opened the faded blue volume that had probably been Aunt Mae's diary. She studied the picture of the oh so thin girl and her soldier.

Maria Ludlov had been very attractive and Shawnee guessed that she had had blond hair, though the black and white picture made it difficult to tell. She remembered her aunt's kind blue eyes and said to herself "Wretched!"

She turned to Grayboy, who seemed to be listening, "Wretched!"

Chapter 10

In the days before her first official day at ERWACHE, Shawnee busied herself with errands that would be more difficult to perform once she started. She knew that Tim had acted to protect her by getting her a position with ERWACHE but still felt uneasy about what her role should be. To help her pass the time prior to that initial Friday night, she did as she was always inclined to do, she thought of others.

Since moving to Covesville to live with Aunt Mae, Shawnee had made few friends but she had met an outgoing high school girl who worked at the CVS pharmacy in the plaza.

Still bothered by that "wretched" comment, she decided to get the picture of Aunt Mae and her soldier enhanced, perhaps even colorized, It was with that intent, that she drove to the CVS to consult with Megan, a senior at Nelson County High.

"I haven't seen you for awhile," Megan began, "is your aunt ok?"

"What? Oh yes, well not really. She had a stroke and then I got married and ..."

"Married?" puzzled the red head. "Who's the lucky guy-I bet he's a hunk!"

"Oh, he is! He's the sweetest..."

"Is that your ring? It's so big and it's so beautiful!"

Shawnee blushed as Megan admired her ring. "Tell me all about it-what's it like, being married and all that?

Shawnee felt the presence of another customer behind her so she felt that she should be brief. "I'll have you come over sometime and we'll talk about my wonderful life."

Megan also now aware of the other customer said, "That's a good idea, now what can we do for you? More medication for your aunt?"

"Well, I'm hoping that this will be a type of medicine that will pick up her spirits. This is a picture of my aunt in 1945 or 1946."

"She was pretty but so skinny," offered Megan.

"I know- I was wondering if you could get it enlarged and maybe colorize it."

"Oh, I'm sure we could. You should see some of my prom pictures-they were terrible until I sent them to Charlottesville. We have our main laboratory there. It'll be Monday before the truck brings it back. Is that ok?"

"That's fine; I hope this will do the trick."

"Me too"-consoled Megan.

Shawnee paid for some rawhide chews for Grayboy and said good-bye to Megan.

Unseen and unheard by Shawnee, was the exchange between Megan and the next customer.

"Excuse me," said the well dressed dark complected stranger." I couldn't help but overhear your conversation with the young woman who just left."

He peered into her brown eyes and she just seemed to melt. (Wow- is he good looking-she almost said out loud).

"I do historical research on World War II- perhaps you've seen the D- Day Memorial at Bedford".

She nodded still entranced by his gaze.

"I know this is highly irregular, but would you allow me to take a picture of the photo that was just turned in. We are always looking for local stories and perhaps I could assist the young lady who just left in picking up her aunt's spirits. Would you allow me to take a quick picture? I have a digital with me and it won't take a moment."

Reflexively, Megan opened the photo-processing envelope and allowed this incredibly handsome man to take two quick pictures of the ancient black and white.

"Thank you," he said, "here is a tip for your trouble."

She looked down as he handed her a ten-dollar bill. His small well-manicured hands stretched from his beautiful French-cuffed shirt. She looked at his unbuttoned collar revealing a dark hairy chest and was about to thank him when the phone rang. She answered the phone quickly putting whoever it was on hold and turned to find him gone.

She shook her head and returned to the phone, "Thank you for holding, how may I help you? No ma'am you just missed her. Yes ma'am, I'll tell her if she comes back in, but I "...

The caller hung up before Megan could finish her statement. She thought to herself –who wears French –cuffs in Nelson County?

Friday afternoon was fast approaching and Shawnee was excited yet nervous about what was expected of her. She had Tim approve her wardrobe-since nothing had been specified by Ingrid. Shawnee and Tim both decided that a nice modest blouse and jeans would probably be fine.

Tim would not get off until after she started work so she made him promise to come to the Lobo's Den as soon as he showered.

She needn't have worried. Despite all of Ingrid's intentions and not a little hype, Friday night's gathering was very small.

In actuality, Ingrid had as much as said so when she had interviewed Shawnee.

Lovingston was a dead town on what was mostly a poorly traveled road. Route 29 stretched between D.C. and Roanoke, two lanes north and south. But Route 29 was flanked on both sides by hopes and dreams that had died. There were a few attempts to revitalize the road, like the trendy Corner Store at North Garden, but that had the advantage of being closer to Charlottesville and wasn't smushed against one side of a mountain where the coal seams had played out like Lovingston was.

Logically then, there wasn't much reason to stop along 29. It came as somewhat of a disappointment that there wasn't much to do on that Friday or the following Saturday night. The local blue grass band that Ingrid tolerated was performing nicely but there just weren't any of "that special clientele" in Ingrid's sights for the first 2 nights.

Dutifully, Tim came to check up on things both nights but the handful of locals were mostly acquaintances of his. He did get to dance with his wife much to her embarrassment.

He was quite good on the dance floor while she was untried.

"You didn't have to pick that song either," she scolded later as they lay in bed.

"What song?" he said pretending not to remember the circumstances surrounding their dance.

"What song? You know very well what song Tim McGregor!"

<u>"If I Said You Have A Beautiful Body Would You Hold It Against Me?"</u>

She pulled away in mock revulsion. "Yes, that one, you know how self conscious I am and ..."

He buried her further words with a deep kiss and all seemingly was forgotten.

Monday morning, Shawnee and Grayboy saw Tim off, straightened up the small home some and headed toward the CVS around 10:00. The wind was picking up a little and she donned her newly issued ERWACHE windbreaker. Hope this wind doesn't push my beetle off the road she thought. In her haste to get back the photo in its newest form, she forgot that Megan wouldn't be there to share it with her. Megan's co-op schedule wouldn't put her there until after 2:00 and it was just now 10:15.

She paid the clerk; an older lady named Thelma, and gingerly opened the envelope.

She was stunned. The photo looked so real. It looked like it could have been taken yesterday. She turned to show the clerk and even though Thelma didn't know the story in detail, she could appreciate the difference between the old and the new.

"That is remarkable. I know your aunt will be thrilled"

"Please thank Megan for me," Shawnee said as she headed toward her bug.

The trip down 29 passed quickly and the bug fought hard against the headwinds of October. She drove into Aunt Mae's yard and then realized that Mae might not be up yet.

She let herself in and met Kristina in the kitchen.

"How's she doing?" asked Shawnee.

The big Samoan smiled and said —"she's fine-she's sleeping now. She sleeps several times a day now usually awake for 2 hours and then sleeps for an hour. You caught me, I was just preparing my prayer list for the week, and your aunt always heads the list. Do you have any prayer concerns?"

Prayer concerns. She hadn't thought about prayer or praying for a long time. The term itself took her back to her parents and the early days on the mission field.

"Why, yes, I have lots of concerns. She confided in Kristina things that she couldn't tell Ingrid and some that she couldn't even tell Tim. How could she protest against a good paying job and a husband that adored her? Yet, it knawed at her that Tim would never come to church with her, even when she pleaded. She so wanted him to develop a spiritual life.

She briefly recounted the days before her wedding when he had consented to attend the Lovingston church with her.

The Lovingston church, the sole survivor of what had been 4 at one time, was staffed by a very proper minister, Gregor Inke. As Shawnee recounted for Kristen, the sermon that the Rev. Inke had preached admonished all Christians to be as Gallio in the Bible.

Kristen offered Shawnee some coffee then puzzled, "Gallio?"

"Gallio. The name didn't ring a bell for me either but when I got back here, Aunt Mae's Bible proved my instincts to be correct.

Gallio, took no position on any controversial issue. My father and mother would have walked out on such nonsense. Tim, on the other hand was afraid I might make a scene if we went back there that is why we got married here in Covesville. I think the Krause's own that church".

"My goodness, I will pray for ...

"Mostly Tim's salvation and then there's the issue of children..."

The friends prayed together and then tiptoed toward the parlor and Aunt Mae's bedside. Shawnee told Grayboy to wait in the hall and she hung up her jacket on the coat tree.

Aunt Mae was glad to see Shawnee but still spoke only a few slurred words.

Shawnee spoke to her while Kristina checked Mae's vital signs. The Lobo's Den and Tim's underground adventures filled most of the time.

"Oh, I almost forgot. I brought you a present. Now close your eyes Aunt Mae. "

That was one of the few things she could do in a coordinated fashion, and she complied.

Shawnee brought out the colorized photo and held it up to get Kristen's approval.

Kristen smiled broadly and nodded the go ahead.

"Ok, open your eyes."

Neither of the women was prepared for Mae's reaction. She lurched forward and gasped, her face formed into what came close to being a smile. She began to cry and sobbed for many minutes thereafter.

Kristina said, "Miss Mae, Shawnee hoped this would lift your spirits."

Aunt Mae struggling to speak said, "Bless you both. Mykke, Mykke"

Neither woman understood exactly what the last two utterances were but Shawnee guessed that her Uncle Mike was what was intended.

They sang **BLESSED ASSURANCE** to Aunt Mae then noticed that she appeared weaker.

"I'll set this here for you to look at" she said as she set it on the nightstand. "Uh, Oh. Look at the time; I need to be going it's later than I thought." She kissed her aunt's forehead and was about to leave the room when Helen entered, carrying lunch on a tray.

"I feared y'all had lost track of time, so I threw together some victuals."

Both Shawnee and Kristina apologized for being so distracted.

"Oh, that's alright. And Grayboy and me took care of that salesman who came to the door looking for you Shawnee. "I tol' him we weren't buying".

"Good for you, thank you" she said as she slipped her windbreaker on and looked one more time in on her aunt.

This time, Aunt Mae seemed to be terrified. She screamed,"AWAKE, AWAKE, pain, pain," then passed out.

The three women looked on in puzzlement.

"Never before" said Kristina.

Chapter 11

If Friday and Saturday nights were going to be slow, Shawnee guessed correctly that Tuesday would absolutely dead. Between four and eight exactly two customers came in, both of them regulars. Shawnee was to learn later that they were 2 of the 3 lawyers that had offices in Lovingston. They briefly spoke to Ingrid, appeared to ogle Shawnee and then settled into playing their on-going chess game. They left at 5: 39 and the rest of the night was quiet.

Shawnee amused herself by surveying the bookshelves and dusting as she went.

Ingrid appeared deep in thought, poring over come company paperwork.

Later that evening, with absolutely no customers to divert them they sat together and watched CNN. The special report on the Middle East violence caused Ingrid to bristle with rage. Shawnee thought it best to remain silent since she couldn't tell whom Ingrid was angry with.

That story was followed by a tragic story of child neglect in Detroit.

Ingrid virtually screamed at the TV set, "Useless **eaters**! That's what those people are. They don't deserve to live."

Shawnee didn't know what to say so she remained silent.

Abruptly, Ingrid sprang to her feet and smiled at Shawnee. "You must forgive me. Some people just bother me. Some would better off to have never drawn breath. Let's talk."

For the next 1 1/2 hours the older woman asked Shawnee a series of questions that made Shawnee even more uncomfortable.

Did she ever look at other men and wonder if she'd made the right choice? How often did she have sex with Tim? Did he satisfy her? Did she believe in abortion? Shawnee was able to dodge most of the questions.

The abortion issue, however, caused Shawnee to finally declare to Ingrid,

"Ingrid, I'm a Christian. The Bible tells us that we are fearfully and wonderfully made in the image of our Creator. I believe that every human life is precious "

"Even if the child is deformed and can never have a normal life? What kind of quality of life could an invalid have?"

She tip- toed around her aunt, remembering the author of that "wretched" label.

"Especially if that was the case."

Drawing as deeply as she could for what she hoped would convince Ingrid that abortion was wrong, she tried tactfully.

"Ingrid, what if there was a woman pregnant for the 5th time who had already given birth to some deformed children and possibly contracted syphilis. Should her 5th child be born or be aborted?"

"Without a doubt –aborted. That should go without argument.
"

"Pardon me for being so rude, Ingrid. but you are from Germany, correct?"

"Yes, yes of course, but what has that to do with the fable you are telling."

Shawnee could feel herself tensing up. Ingrid was growing increasingly agitated. Time to finish the story.

"If you had aborted the 5th child you would have aborted Beethoven."

Silence. Just silence. Both women knew that Shawnee had just won the point, game, match and set.

Ingrid's cold blue eyes glared at the younger woman.

Finally, Ingrid said. "You may go. Be here Friday at 4".

"Yes ma'am," Shawnee said. She quickly grabbed her windbreaker and headed toward the door. "Good night".

There was continued silence from the blond German who had made Shawnee so tense throughout the evening.

"Thank you Mom and Dad and especially thank you Jesus," she said aloud. Shawnee literally floated to the Volkswagen, particularly happy that she could spend some time with Tim before he had to get to sleep.

"You should have been there. I had her on the ropes ", Shawnee crowed as she did her best Rocky Balboa impersonation, playfully sparring with the unsuspecting Tim.

Her dancing and jabbing caused Grayboy to get up and try to play with her. She grabbed his front paws and continued to dance with him for several minutes.

"I just don't like to be talked down to. She's so self-righteous. I don't care if she is rich- they don't have children- how can she be so cold?"

Tim had no answer for that question.

"Come here champ but take off the gloves."

They cuddled up as the wind picked up outside.

"Timmy, don't forget 2 weeks from tomorrow is our mini-honeymoon."

"How could I forget?"

The next week and a half flew by. The "talk" that Ingrid and Shawnee had had seemed to be forgotten, or at least never mentioned. Ingrid seemed cordial and on occasion even jovial as she too looked forward to the company holiday on October 29th.

Since it was mostly just the two of them at the Lobo's Den, they had time to talk but it was only light banter and never for very long.

Shawnee dedicated herself to planning the perfect get-a-way. She researched the Peaks of Otter Inn using the computer at the Lobo's Den. Perfect she thought. No phones, romantic atmosphere, good price, well within Virginia, he can even fish some.

Next she decided to round up all the "special effects" she would need: bubble bath, candles-maybe even a scented candle or 2, perfume, a new night gown?

She wanted to surprise Tim so she kept all of her plans to herself- not telling even Helen or Kristen.

She did need some help in the "special effects" department but who should she ask? Certainly not Ingrid. Maybe Megan- sure Megan gave good advice about the picture, and she'd know a lot probably about what kind of perfume to get.

Shawnee went to the CVS on the Monday before their trip. She waited until after 2 PM and sure enough her friend was there manning the register.

They talked excitedly between the few customers and Megan seemed just as pumped up for Shawnee getting to go as Shawnee was.

"Now this one is a man-slayer", she said as they whiffed the exotic aroma of Spring Dawn perfume. "My older sister has caught some big ones with this."

"*Some*?"

"Yeah, she likes to play the field."

"Well. my field is all set and I think this stuff may just work, thanks."

"Where are you going to play the vamp?"

"Vamp?"

"Vamp, enchantress, you know, to seduce him?"

"Seduce my husband?"I really hadn't thought of it in those terms. Anyway, Peaks of Otter Inn-but keep it hush- hush, ok?

"Promise, besides who would I tell anyway, Thelma? "

"Thanks- remember, we have to get together sometime, ok.

On Monday and Tuesday, she busied herself with trip preparations and arranged for Grayboy to stay at Aunt Mae's. She consulted with Helen and Kristen and both thought it good idea that Grayboy stay with Mae. She was alone from 9 pm to almost 9 every morning since social services would only pay for 2 shifts. It had crossed Shawnee's mind that later on she might come each morning after Tim left for work, but so far, the arrangement seemed to be working.

Tuesday at the Lobo's Den was just as slow as ever and she just couldn't wait to get home. She could not believe Ingrid kept the place open until 5:35, then finally relented and closed up early.

Tim was entrusted with more responsibility than ever and now had to carry a pager. He had promised Shawnee that he wouldn't need the pager on the company day off. True to his word, he met her at the door of their humble home and laid down his pager and coveralls.

She jumped all over him and grabbed his hand. She swooped down and picked up the light travel bag, nudging him toward the small suitcase she had packed.

"I'll drive," she proclaimed.

" Only if you promise no more 140 mile per hour time trials"- he cautioned as he held the keys to the truck out of the reach of his now leaping 5 foot 8 inch wife.

She went for his mid-section, causing him to lower the keys and she snatched them.

"You pays your money, you takes your chances," she mocked.

"Seriously, keep it under 70. Promise?"

"Where's your sense of adventure, McGregor? Oh, ok, you did say 80 didn't you?"

"I said 75"- he offered weakly, realizing that she had won

They stopped for a burger and malt at Colleen and then she drove rapidly toward Bedford.

Peaks of Otter Inn was exactly as she had hoped quaint but not antiquated and definitely romantic. They checked in and showed themselves to the large room with 2 double beds. Each room had an elevated porch overlooking the twin peaks now illuminated by the half moon. Just below their room, there was a stretch of lawn that ended perhaps 50 feet further at the edge of a large man-made lake. They just breathed in the beauty of the scene and watched the deer, now boldly munching on the grass just below their porch.

"They don't look real"-mused Shawnee.

"The only thing unreal is you. You're too good to be true", he said holding her tightly.

Their first night was absolutely perfect. With no phone, TV or pager, not even Grayboy. They enjoyed just being there together, alone, re-igniting their honeymoon trip that had been so joyous until they we blindsided by that call to come back to Virginia.

She fell asleep in the comforting arms of her Tim. She loved him so and she felt equally loved. Aunt Mae was being well cared for. Both McGregors were now employed though she didn't really enjoy her job, she knew that it was Tim's wish that she work there and that it did help keep her mind off of Aunt Mae "Thank you, God, for blessing me," she whispered as she drifted off to sleep.

She let Tim sleep in the next morning. She decided to serve him breakfast in bed. She slipped on her sweat suit and headed to the restaurant at the far end of the Inn. She was surprised that so few people were about until she saw the clock- 7:18. It was foggy and damp but the air was so fresh. She gloried in just being here with her love.

She took some samples of all that was on the breakfast bar back to their room. He slept until 8:29 when she looked in on him from the porch.

She absolutely smothered him with affection and then fed him.

Tim was just about to doze off when she grabbed his big toe and said, "Ok, nap time is over- up and at'em".

"At who? – come back to bed, I'll make it worth your while" – he teased.

"All play and no work isn't good for you"-she countered.

"No work? I work hard every day-I thought this is honeymoon part 2!"

"It is, but we have to spend time working on our marriage."
Puzzled, Tim sat up and scratched his head." Are we in trouble?
Is there someone else?"
"Not on this planet!"- She said running to him and hugging him
for all she was worth.
"It's just- promise not to get mad?"
He nodded.
"Do you know what I've been doing while you slept?"
He shook his head.
"I've been reading the Gideon Bible –the one in the drawer by
the bed. Tim we have a great relationship I think but it could be
so much deeper if believed the same thing about God."
Up to this point, he listened carefully but she sensed that she
had once again crossed the line.
"How about this? Let's not talk about this anymore today.
Let's go see God's handiwork. You spend so much of your time
underground, let me show you what God has done on the surface
–it's so beautiful here- get dressed and let me show you."
Tim figured what was there to lose- if it pleased her to walk
around and see the sites that was ok. He did want to make her
happy but this God stuff... it must really mean something to
her. Well here goes...
They enjoyed their day together. Here he was with the most
beautiful girl he had ever seen. Her every move was beauty.
She cared about nature, she loved the outdoors. She coddled
a sparrow that they found with a broken wing. She acted like
she wanted to take it back and mother it back to health, but she
surprised him by telling the sparrow:
"Don't worry little bird, our heavenly Father knows about you
and he will take care of you." She handed him to Tim- "Put that
6 foot 4 inch frame of yours to use and set our small friend back
in this cedar tree. "
Tim complied.
They walked over the mountain terrain, hand in hand- laughing
and kissing frequently. By a small waterfall, they ate the picnic
lunch she had packed, enjoying the silence and loving the time
spent together.

As dusk approached, they headed back toward the inn. She excused herself and headed first to the restaurant, then quickly to the room.

She ran to him where she had left him, by the pond. She handed him a brand new fishing pole to replace the one she had "lost".

"Now you stay here and fish while I prepare your evening's entertainment," she said with a wink.

Thirty minutes later, having caught 2 non-keepers Tim headed toward the room and the one he knew he *would* keep. He entered the room and was greeted by the intoxicating smell of vanilla candles burning at three places in the room. Shawnee was nowhere in sight. He sat on the bed and took off his shoes and socks. There was some form of food on the table and he was about to investigate when the bathroom door opened. More marvelous smells. He got up and headed toward the door only to see more candles and a fully drawn bubble bath. His bride peeked from behind the door and took his hand, leading him toward the tub. She climbed in and waited for him to disrobe.

Suddenly, there was a knock on the front door of their room. She ducked under the bubbles and he answered the door hesitatingly.

She heard only part of the conversation.

"Yes" he was Tim McGregor.... "Just a minute"- he left their room with someone.

Tim returned grimly a few minutes later.

"Honey, the desk clerk just got a call for us. You, really. That was Ingrid. She said she's been trying to find us all day. It's about Mae, she's... we need to drive home tonight."

The call was brief.

"Done?"

"Yes, sir."

"Complications?"

"Just the dog- I doped him and tied him outside- I did the job and left. You were correct sir."

"About?"
"1409-2."
"Who never existed?"
"Correct."

Chapter 12

They didn't talk much on the way home. Both of them had been kind of expecting the news sooner or later. It just seemed so bizarre that Mae would pass now.

Tim's pick-up gobbled up the road as they sped toward Covesville.

At the house, the McGregor's met the Nelson County sheriff, Helen, and Grayboy.

Shawnee said, "Helen, thank you so much for being here. Did you find her?"

"No ma'am. Kristina found her here this morning. Grayboy was barking and she felt something was very wrong. The strange thing is that I left Grayboy with Miss Mae last night and he was tied up outside this morning, raisin' Cain".

"Which brings me into the picture, Mrs. McGregor. I am Terry Sullivan with the Sheriff's department. I hate to ask but could you please view the body for a positive id?"

He drew the sheet back and the McGregors and Helen all concurred.

Mae looked so peaceful. Just like she was asleep.

"Is everything as you expected?" the deputy asked.

What is that mark on her forearm?" Tim asked

The deputy slowly turned the dead woman's forearm.

What Tim had seen was part of the first of five crudely etched numbers that Mae bore on her arm.

"Look's to be a tattoo. Probably quite old. Have any of you ever noticed them before?

Helen spoke up- "Yes sir, I saw them when I bathed her but I never could ask her in her condition".

Shawnee felt ashamed that she had never noticed.

"What do the numbers mean? ", Shawnee ventured.

"I'm not sure. It looks to me like 1 or is that a 7? Then 4 ,0,9 and maybe 2 or is that a Z?" asked Tim.

"As I stated earlier, the tattoo looks quite old. I don't personally believe that there is any connection to your aunt's death. We will just record the death as being of natural causes unless you want an autopsy. Both health care providers say that everything looks as it should. Nothing missing, is there Mrs. McGregor?"

"I don't think so," she said as she retreated to the shelter of Tim's arms.

Just down the hill from Aunt Mae's house, across the tracks and on the other side of the Covesville Presbyterian Church education building, two men sat in the back of a gray panel van. The van was specially equipped for night surveillance. Both men had listened intently to the conversation that just ended in the dead woman's parlor.

"See I told you the house was clean."

"But they found the proof we were looking for, on Frau Ludlov's arm. Why didn't we think to check there?"

"Is the number alone enough for further investigation?"

"The number is certainly more than we had but there must be more –perhaps that photo..."

"But we have run the photo. We have only the soldiers' first name and little else."

"Perhaps my friend at the pharmacy. She and the girl are friends- perhaps the photo is one of many, or even a journal."

Their conversation was ended by the convoy leaving Covesville. Nicholson's funeral home's hearse lead the procession, followed by Helen's Tempo, the McGregor's truck, now with Grayboy on board, and Sheriff Sullivan.

It was after 1:30 am before Tim got them home. He checked the answering machine in hopes that Ingrid or Dr. Jo might have granted Tim the day off. There were no messages.

"I just can't believe they couldn't give you the day off. There is so much to do. When my parents died, I didn't have to arrange their funeral- I don't know what to do. Where should she be buried? Here in Lovingston is out of the question."

"Why?"

"Tim, it's a spiritual thing. That Right Reverend Inke is not the man I need. They might as well hang Ichabod over the church door"

"Trace, it's late- I don't want you to fret. Couldn't that Filipino caregiver, what's her name-Jane...?

"She's Samoan and its Kristina- but you are right-she is the best one to talk to. I'm so sorry Timmy, it's so late- please get to bed. 4:30 comes so soon."

He kissed and hugged her and in 10 minutes was sound asleep.

Shawnee petted Grayboy and those big brown eyes brought her a degree of comfort. What to do, what to do?

She thought it best to write down a plan for later that morning. She took a piece of notebook paper and absently slid the faded blue book under it for a writing surface.

To do: flowers/ burial site/death certificate/funeral service/ pastor/legal stuff-who can help?

Ask Helen or Kristina for help.

She looked at her sleeping husband. They had been interrupted twice now on their honeymoon but that didn't seem important now. He had shown strength through the night's ordeal but she knew he could not know how she felt about her Aunt's death. She stroked Grayboy's head and prayed softly:

"Dear Lord, thank you for receiving Aunt Mae and please tell her I miss her already. Lord, I am joyous tonight that she is no longer suffering and that she is safe in Jesus' arms. I want to lift up my husband Tim. Help him to awake up to you Lord, help him to see that Mae's home going is the start, not the end of everything. I am asking in Jesus' name that you convict Tim of the need to be saved. I love him and I pray that he will see through me even a tiny bit of the love that Jesus has for all of us. Thank you for loving me, even when I am unlovely towards others. Forgive me of my sins, especially of the feelings I have toward the Krause's right now. Lord help me to be the supportive wife I need to be.

Now that it is late-, I ask for strength that I know you will provide-help me to sleep quickly, to rise early to feed Timmy and sustain me through the days ahead. These things I ask in the name above all names, Jesus, my lord, Amen."

She set her notes in the book and snuggled down into the big armchair for what would pass for a 2-hour nap.

She was already cooking her pancake fried apple special when Tim's alarm went off at 4:30.

He dressed quickly and moved to hug her but she hugged him first.

"Trace are you ok? Did you sleep any?"

She held him close and nodded her head. A sleepy, "I'm fine". was all she said.

"I'm going to see if they will let me off or at least maybe I can come home early"...- he started.

"Don't worry- there really isn't that much to do. What's today-Friday?"

"Thursday".

"I guess maybe the funeral should be Friday or would Saturday be better?"

"Saturday- I'm off and can help you more."

"Ok, here's your lunch"- she held on tightly for one last moment.

"Shawnee, I love you." He kissed her sweetly then retreated toward the door. "Please get some sleep"

She nodded and hopped into bed.

As Tim hurried toward work, he kept thinking to himself, 'I need to do more for that girl'. Maybe I can finish the coupe by Christmas- maybe we can really go somewhere each weekend. As he turned into the parking lot he spoke to the first man he saw. No response.

The tram was pretty much silent as well.

A tired Tim McGregor began his 11-hour shift with a headache that only sleep could cure. He napped for the 10 minutes it took for the tram to get him to the coal veins and awoke with a start. Yawning, Tim made his way toward the time clock. He moved toward the underground train that would take him 300 feet down to the site of Tuesday's job. He checked his headlamp, beeper, and oxygen mask. Everything was go. He sat on the auger, checked his watch. 5:58 am. Before he turned it on, he tried to remember why the word Ichabod kept rattling around in his mind.

Shawnee slept until 9:15 and then remembered that today was not going to be a normal one. She showered, played briefly with Grayboy, then sat down to make some phone calls. The social services agency was hesitant at first to divulge Kristina's home phone number but something in Shawnee's voice and her sincere plea soon had it for her.

"Kristina? - Hi, this Shawnee, I just wanted to thank..."

"Shawnee- you don't need to thank me for anything. I'm just sorry I couldn't stay until you got home. Your Aunt was so sweet; the last thing she did was recite the 23rd Psalm with Helen. We both felt she was slipping away so we sang to her and read her Bible to her. She was really at peace-she sure looked at peace when I found her."

"I'm sorry I didn't tell you where we were going, maybe things would have been..."

"Don't give it a thought. The Lord called her home and she was ready-rest assured of that."

"It's just that there's so much I feel I should have done and could have done while she was healthy- I don't know where to turn for legal advice- did she have a will, where did she want to be buried, so much more."

"How about I meet you at the house in an hour- would that give you enough time to gather your thoughts and we can work on some of these problems."

"Kristina, isn't it closer for you to come here, aren't you close to the Tye River Church?"

"Yes, but I don't want to put you out any...'

"Nonsense, please come here. You'll be my first house guest!"

"An hour then?"

"Done. Take care on your way here. Oh- how about some directions? You can take the second entrance to Lovingston, come up a block and turn left. Look for the smallest stone cottage you've ever seen. Or if you come to the entrance off of 29, come up a block and turn right, look for the Volkswagen out front".

"Ok, see you then".

Shawnee in her tired state was never so grateful for their tiny home. It took 10 minutes to straighten up the entire place.

As she waited for Kristina, she nodded in the overstuffed easy chair.

Grayboy announced Kristina's arrival, or at least his barking made her think so.

She opened the front door to see only a gray van down the street. Grayboy continued barking from his back yard vantage point until she let him in and even then, he seemed restless. She offered to play ball but he was distracted so instead she put some coffee on and waited for her friend.

True to her word, the large Samoan, Shawnee's sister in Christ, arrived at precisely the agreed upon time. They hugged and prayed with other and then got down to resolving the many issues that faced the 22-year-old niece.

"Where should I have her buried?"

"Well, I imagine that the Covesville Church would be her choice," offered Kristina.

Lifting the phone, she called Pastor Tyler, the pastor who had married them, and slowly laid out her thoughts.

"I was hoping you might do the service for her.. You can! ... I see –I was thinking about 10:00 am-ok- Oh that would be so nice of you...and I think she would like to be buried there or at the house. Oh, I see, I hadn't really thought about that, that is a problem- and the house? Uh-huh..., yes, yes, I see. That would take time then, No., not that I know of at least. Ok. Thank you-Nicholson's 1-3 probably on Friday. Thank you again-yes, I will when he gets home –he's probably ½ mile down by now. Yes, sir, God Bless you too."

"I heard some uh-ohs in that conversation- what did he say".

"The service is fine, they even have a bagpiper in their congregation- I know she would've loved that-maybe Amazing Grace, **BUT** she can't be buried there, the graveyard has been closed down since 1985 and there just isn't a way around that."

"Where do they bury their congregation then?"

"He suggested Charlottesville or some other local church yard".

"Maybe here "... she started but Shawnee's shaking head stopped her." Oh, that's right, but you wouldn't have to talk to this, what's his name?"

"Inke. But he'd probably have to approve it –no that's not an option."

"How about at the house?"

"Well, he asked if there was a will and if not there would be a lengthy process that even then might have the house go to the state of Virginia and that could get sticky."

"I think she'd feel at home at the Tye River Church-with your parents..."

"That was my best hope- I can't see Charlottesville or here- who do I have to have to talk to at your church? "

"We have a deacon board that I'm sure will let you bury her near your folks-we haven't had a steady pastor for about 2 years but we're looking. Here-let me call for you."

Within 30 minutes, she had her answer. The board would certainly welcome Mae's internment and apologized for not having a regular pastor to comfort the family.

"One more thing, Shawnee, they, are all so grateful for the service that that your folks gave to the church, there will be no charge. They will take care of the digging and grounds keeping-no charge."

"Just like Jesus! He paid it all"

They were in prayer when Tim came home. He wasn't rude just soooo tired –he listened patiently to the schedule of events that had been set up and sat down wearily on the bed.

"That sounds good-thank you Kristina for all of your help- I'm sorry I couldn't be here. I can't believe they couldn't excuse me."

"I'm going to do one more thing for you two"- proclaimed the Samoan. "I'm going up to the plaza, and bring you some McDonald's for dinner-it's not much but both of you need to rest."

With that, she left.

The couple embraced and lay side by side on their big feather mattress.

"Trace, I'm so sorry about all this..., I should be here".

"Shhhh, she said-just rest, I know you would if you could at least tomorrow is ...FRIDAY-she sat bolt upright-Timmy- you don't think that Ingrid will make me work do you?"

"I wish I could tell you no, but unfortunately, tomorrow is also one of ERWACHE's "big" days. Ingrid always insists that people come to the Lobo's Den for Halloween- the Krauses are really into it."

"Halloween!??? I just don't think I can ..."

With the knock on the door came dinner and finally rest.

Hours later, she couldn't stop thinking –"Halloween- Lord what kind of people are these?"

Chapter 13

She awoke at the alarm but Tim was already up and dressed. He sat down on the bed and comforted her.

"Today is going to be a long one for you so stay in bed. Doctor's orders!" he said, kissing her forehead. "I've set the alarm for 10:30. Now promise me you'll rest."

She shook her head "but it just isn't right- you work so hard and ..."

"Don't worry- rest- promise?"

"Ok."

He kissed her good bye and patted Grayboy on the head. He motioned to the dog to guard his woman and without a moments' hesitation, the dog laid down in front of the bed.

On his way to work, he thought about what she was facing today, alone. She would have to endure the viewing of her Aunt's body from 1-3. He couldn't be there with her because some people in China or India were waiting for him to harvest coal. Where was the justice in all this? Had the company sent a card or even called beyond the call to come home? Of course, the funeral was still a day away; they'll probably send flowers- still how is any of this right?

He descended from his truck and spoke to the first person he saw, a younger man with a full head of red hair. The man nodded and kept going. Tim mused, "at least he heard me".

His schedule for the day sent him back toward where Auger 12 had broken through into the auto graveyard. He had reported it but not thought about it since then. Maybe that VW face down in the pool of water would help him restore her bug. She would probably like her beetle restored. His mind raced back to her. She is going to have such along trying 2 days, working both nights, the funeral service, the Halloween party tonight. How can I make it up to her?

Several miles away and several hundred feet above the mine, Shawnee awakened with the sound of the alarm.
She stretched, let Grayboy out back and showered. As she showered, she began to think of what lay ahead. No wonder Ingrid was so chipper on Tuesday. She wasn't excited about the holiday, it was this Halloween party. "Oh, Lord sustain me"-she prayed.
  She called the funeral home to see what was needed and then put on her most modest dress. After making sure that Grayboy had food and water, she traveled to Nicholson's.
The visiting hours were from 1-3. She arrived a little after 12 and met briefly with the funeral home owner, Proctor Nicholson. They chatted briefly and concluded the paper work regarding the costs for casket, embalming and use of the facility. $2678.00 later, she thought to herself, Tim said to go ahead and pay for it-but I'll make it up to him with my job.
Her season of mourning was virtually unpunctuated. Besides Helen and Kristina, only Pastor Tyler came to be with her. The Tye River congregation sent the only flowers. 2 cards were presented from the Covesville church but no visitors.
As the viewing hours concluded, Shawnee thanked everyone at the parlor and headed toward her car. She had brought a change of clothes so that she could head straight to work. She changed in the restroom of the funeral home and surprised Mr. Nicholson and his small staff by her transformation back into jeans.

She thought to herself all the way there- I just cannot believe not one thing from the Krauses, and now I have to go into this, this party and pretend that everything is normal.

Her worst fears were realized when she arrived shortly before 4 pm. The interior of the Lobo's Den resembled a bat cave, or what she thought a bat cave would look like. Cobwebs, creepy things hanging down- gross plastic puddles lying around. The normal background music had been replaced by sound effects of screams and chains rattling accompanied by an eerie pipe organ.

She was glad she saw all this stuff in daylight –it would be really depressing at night. She stepped outside and prayed quickly to herself,

"Finally, brethren, whatsoever things are true, whatsoever things are honest, whatsoever things are just, whatsoever things are pure, whatsoever things are lovely, whatsoever things are of good report: if there be any virtue, and if there be any praise, think on these things. - Philippians 4:8- she recited to her invisible parents. Thanks again, Mom and Dad."

As yet, she had not seen Ingrid but would not have known her had she not been looking for her. She was dressed in full costume as a witch. She had also been hitting the beer supply by the slur of her words.

"SOOO good to see you Shawnee, you look especially pretty. Have a drink?"

"No thank you. What do you need me to do?"

"Do? What do you ever need to do? Just stand around and look fetching."

At that moment a fully dressed Dracula figure came by- he stopped and ogled Shawnee.

"And who do we have here?" he puzzled.

"That's Tim's wife –you remember Jo- the wedding."

"Oh yes, you look so different –in a good way –Wow, I didn't recall your chest, er.. figure..." He was stumbling as the alcohol was twisting his words.

"I believe I'll sweep the front porch if that's, ok. -offered Shawnee.

"Certainly my dear cackled the witch, you can use my broom!"
She and the vampire laughed rudely as Shawnee walked out.
It was just growing dark and she could see a little movement on
the Lovingston streets among the few houses that had children.
Soon, the distant echoes of trick or treat were obscured by
the arrival sounds of several cars. Those arriving were all in
costume- from knights to ghouls to ballerinas and gypsies.
These were the higher brow society of old Lovingston, plus
some of the local wine growers.
She thought to herself, I know Tim is tired but I sure need him
here. He had promised to come as soon as he could so she made
herself busy waiting on tables and serving the guests. There
were several passes made at her and someone had actually
grabbed her on the bottom.
She hated all of this. Where was the good to cling to in any of
this?
She looked up at about 8:00 pm and saw a really beautiful
girl walk in alone and not in costume. This girl was blonde
and exceptionally well proportioned. She also appeared a little
unsure of what she was seeing.
"Hi, I'm Carly Addison," she said shaking Shawnee's hand. "I
saw the sign out on Route 29 so I thought I'd see what the locals
do for fun."
"Sign on Route 29?"
"Yes, there was this arrow sign pointing to this place that simply
said *PARTY*, so here I am. I just finished grad school at UVA and
I was headed home-or at least where home is now. I'm going to
be working in Roanoke. I'm originally from California."
"Is that your Jeep?" -Shawnee posed, pointing to the gleaming
yellow CJ with the black bikini top.
"Why yes. My folks gave it to me for finishing grad school. Say it
looks like you and I are the only ones not in costume-will they
mind if I stay?"
Her answer came not from Shawnee but from the Krauses
who pounced on this truly beautiful girl and seemed overly
interested in her.

"This is Carly Addison," Shawnee shouted over the groans being broadcast over the PA. "She just graduated from UVA. She is…"

"So nice of you to drop by," interrupted Ingrid. "This is my husband Dr. Josef Krause".

Carly and Dr. Jo instantly got into the 'who do you know at UVA game' as Ingrid continued to study the newcomer.

"Get our guest a drink. Do you prefer wine or rum punch? We have a number of local wineries- would you like me to pick one for you?"

Carly nodded as the Monster Mash played in the background.

"Get her the Wilson # 18'" she commanded of Shawnee.

Shawnee dutifully served the new arrival and Carly was whisked away to meet the partygoers.

It was now approaching 8:30 and Shawnee was so relieved that this madness would end at 10:00, if Ingrid kept her word. Big if, she thought. Where is Timmy?

At precisely that moment, Tim entered and she flew to his side.

"I have never been more glad to see you," she shouted over the now playing Addams Family theme.

They hugged each other and headed toward the porch. Their time together was short lived as Ingrid insisted that they come inside. Tim wasn't in costume but he was quickly introduced all around, this time to the ladies.

Carly somehow shook loose from the mob that was now involved in some circle dance and returned to Shawnee.

"Wow, I just barely escaped. There are some really wild and crazy people out there. One man grabbed my breast."

"I wonder if that is the same man who grabbed…"

"Hey, who is that hunk by the vampire?" Carly cut in. "I sure wouldn't mind meeting him!"

The irony was killing Shawnee. Here she was among the people she least wanted to be around, being asked to be an attraction, and here was this wild party, getting wilder by the minute, with people ogling her husband.

She barely managed to keep her composure as she announced, "That's my husband."

"Really? He is so handsome! Want to share him?"

Stunned, Shawnee simply said, "Not a chance!" Who would ask such a question?

"Well if you ever change your mind..." she couldn't finish because a man dressed up as a Nazi, took her by the hand and led her to the dance floor.

Tim having been introduced all around and his attraction now being replaced by Carly's sensual dancing, escaped to Shawnee.

"Tim, I can't stand this. This is paganism. "

He took her outside to console her and she was just beginning to tell him of the outrages of the last hour when they realized they were not alone on the porch. From over in the dark corner, it was obvious that some sort of sexual activity was occurring right there in the open.

She quickly stormed off the porch and headed toward the parked cars, stopping by Carly's brand new yellow jeep.

There she was finally able to compose herself and tell Tim of what she had seen.

"Timmy, I absolutely hate this. I am quitting right now if they won't let me leave. This place, this party, is evil. Please go in and tell Ingrid I'm sick. I cannot stand this another minute. Please."

He promised he would and he returned to the porch. Whatever was going on in the corner seemed to be escalating.

He entered the party and ran into Rolf, Dr. Jo's number 2 man. He quickly explained the situation and Rolf made no sign of even hearing him. Tim added, "By the way, would you ask Dr. Jo if I can have that old bug in Shaft 16." This time Rolf shrugged and walked away. Tim seemed to be getting nowhere.

The crowd was watching Carly on stage dancing ever more wildly.

Out of the corner of his eye, Tim found Ingrid holding up the bar. She appeared well past drunk.

As he approached her, she grabbed him and kissed him hard on the lips.

He quickly pulled away.

"Timmy!" What's wrong? Don't you want some drink to more?"

"Ingrid, I am taking Shawnee home- she has the funeral tomorrow and..."

"Funeral, smuneral, who died anyway? Say look at that girl- she's really hot!" He glanced at the stage where 2 men were now dancing with Carly. "Stick around, Timmy, we just got started..."

It was obvious that there was nothing left for him to say.

He tried one more time but she just flicked her wrist at him like go away.

As Tim headed toward the door, he glanced at the clock over the door- 9:56. At least Shawnee fulfilled her expected hours.

She was still at Carly's yellow Jeep, now leaning on it.

He grabbed her hand and walked her quickly toward the truck.

On the way home, he apologized for the trauma she had experienced and for not having gotten there sooner. She said nothing.

Tim unlocked the door and led her into their home. She was amazed. Tim had completely repainted the interior in her favorite color, peach. The curtains still needed replacing but she turned to him and kissed him.

"Thank you so much-this is why you were late getting there tonight- you *were* thinking of me all along."

He turned her toward the mantle and pointed out the flowers in the new vase.

"Oh Timmy, you are so thoughtful. "

"I try to be," he said hugging her.

"Oh no, I forgot my purse!" she cried. I so much wanted to leave- do you think I should go back and get it?"

"No. You...we, have along day ahead tomorrow ... you go on to bed; I'll run back and get it".

"I'll be waiting for you," she winked.

Tim hopped in the truck and quickly returned to the scene of what his wife had described as the crimes.

There was now, no crowd. As he entered the Lobo's Den, only 3 people were visible. Ingrid, Dr. Jo and Carly.

Carly seemed to be really out of it. The other two glanced up and glared at Tim.

"Yes?" demanded Ingrid.

"Shawnee left her purse".

"Then get it and please leave".

As Tim headed for the kitchen, he heard Dr. Jo and Ingrid talking in what were normal tones. The screeching background music of the early evening had now been replaced by country music. He was reaching into Shawnee's locker, when Rolf pushed by him on his way to the Krauses.

Tim was about to go, but decided to get a drink of water. As he drank, the strains of "she walks these hills in a long black veil" wafted over the intercom.

He placed the drinking glass in the sink and reentered the Espresso bar where the Krauses were still hovering over Carly.

"Is she ok?" –Tim inquired.

"Oh yes, she's going to be fine"- responded ERWACHE's founder.

Suddenly Carly jerked. It was totally involuntary. She looked to Tim to be convulsing.

Dr.Krause quickly laid her out on the floor, while Ingrid brought pillows to surround her with.

Tim asked "Are you sure I can't help?"

"No, no. She will be fine- she must be an epileptic," Dr. Krause stated calmly. We well get her to the infirmary. You may go".

As he headed toward the door, a very sober Ingrid said- "Tim, we will not be open tomorrow night, I'd like Shawnee to come and clean up only. After that, she may leave."

Tim nodded and opened the door, as the strains of Long Black Veil ended, *Nobody knows, nobody sees, nobody knows but me.*

He thought about the events of the last 3 hours for it was just now after 11. His bosses' wife had kissed him, his wife was so sickened by what she saw at work that she demanded to leave, and this Carly girl having survived the wildness of the party, now lay in convulsions. Tomorrow looked a little brighter – at least Shawnee didn't have to endure more of the same.

He finished the short drive, locked his truck and opened the door to their home. The lights were low but she was already sleeping soundly. She looked so sweet- my angel he thought. There was no point of waking her-she needed rest. He sat in the easy chair and absently opened the faded blue book that had Mae's picture in it. Inside the book he found and read Shawnee's to do list regarding the funeral. She had covered everything. She was so considerate. Always thinking of others before herself- there was really something to this Golden Rule stuff he thought...He was surprisingly not tired, so he thumbed through Mae's book- I wonder if someone could translate this for us- maybe the Krauses he mused. HMMM, no time soon though...He closed the small book and looked at the beautiful girl that was his wife. Carly was pretty, some would say a knockout, but Shawnee was beautiful -in every way. He just sat there and watched her breathe. What did I do to deserve her he thought? How can I show her she's my everything? He thought about the million little things she did. That silly Brad Paisley song rolled through his mind, *I Live, For, Little Moments, Like That*...He glanced at the clock- barely now midnight.

Tim jumped up and tiptoed toward the front door. He reached into her purse and got her keys. He would clean up, tonight!

He decided to walk back to the Lobo's Den. The place was now lit by just a few interior lights.

He noticed that Carly's jeep was still parked outside but was relieved to find no one inside- indeed everything was shut down.

He set himself to cleaning the place and was overcome by the enormous task that lay ahead. The smell of spilled drinks was nowhere near as bad as the puddles of vomit he found in 5 places. He found drink glasses everywhere, a few had been broken. He mopped up the spills and vacuumed the few-carpeted areas. He realigned the sofas and chairs and disinfected every area he could think of. He adjusted the cushions and was shocked to find a pair of women's panties in the sofa.

It was now pushing 2 am hard. He had finished all but the kitchen and then remembered the front porch would need sweeping at least.

There was a smashed pumpkin on the porch floor and under it; Tim found an empty condom wrapper. He was reviled by this and at the same time so glad he was doing the cleaning not Shawnee.

Tim finished the porch by hosing it down. It was not yet cold enough in Virginia to worry about ice so he figured the water would help cleanse this mess.

He took a quick look at the windows and removed the few seasonal decorations that were taped there. No need to wash the windows-at least not in this light- he'd check them tomorrow-tomorrow was now today- Saturday morning. It was close to 3 now and the kitchen remained to finish. After another 45 minutes of arduous labor, the trash was in the dumpster, the dishes done, the floor mopped and he considered everything finished.

He locked up and was headed home when he noticed that the yellow Jeep was nowhere to be seen. He thought about that and the night's other bizarre events- all this seemed too weird- he needed to talk to Shawnee but he also knew that he needed to be strong for her today.

He entered the house. Grayboy met him at the door and Tim briefly greeted him.

He set the alarm for 8, a scant 3 ½ hours from now. The service was to be at Covesville at 10 and burial at Tye River afterwards, he remembered from her notes. At least she could rest afterward now that he had covered for her at the Lobo's Den.

It seemed to Tim that the alarm went off 10 minutes later.

She was already dressed in her darkest dress. He surveyed his bride. Even in mourning dress, she was so wonderful to watch.

"Come on Tim," she intoned; I'd like us to be early".

He got up, a little more weary than usual. They were fed and on the road to Covesville by 9:00.

She didn't say much this morning and he figured she was focused on the funeral. She however was trying to understand what she had seen at the hands of the Krauses last night.

The small church had may have had 15 members total. Almost all were Mae's age; even Pastor Tyler had long ago retired. This was a dying church but enough of the gospel message was being preached that Shawnee had enjoyed coming here. Along with the small congregation, a few from Tye River had come, as well as Helen and Kristina.

Tim saw very few tears as Mae's life was recounted.

"Never missing a **Sunday** for 52 years, until her stroke. Faithful in her tithe. Helping where she could. She had volunteered to help search for the victims of Hurricane Camille. Although we never found the citizens of Massie's Mill, Maria Ludlov cared for others." Pastor Tyler encouraged everyone to be as faithful as Mae had been.

The service was centered on the 23rd Psalm:

The Lord is my shepherd,
I shall not want,
He maketh me to lie down in green pastures,
He leadth me beside the still waters,
He restoreth my soul,
He leadth me in the paths of righteousness for His name sake,
Yea, though I walk through the valley of the shadow of death,
I will fear no evil, for thou art with me,
Thy rod and thy staff they comfort me.

Tim listened as the congregation recited the rest of the verse in unison from memory...

"and I shall dwell in the house of the Lord forever".

79

Amen was repeated by all and the service ended with
Bless be the tie that binds,
Our hearts in Christian love,
The fellowship of Kindred minds,
Is like to that above.

Tim was amazed that the small group had sung and repeated the verses from memory. There seemed to be a joy to this service he had not expected.

They drove to the Tye River Church, led by Deputy Sheriff Sullivan.

There the service was brief and the crowd small; at least from the Covesville congregation-few had made the trip. However, 20 or so greeted the McGregors after Mae was prayed over and the funeral ended. This small congregation of Kristina's church welcomed everyone in to have something to eat.

Tim had not expected anything like this. He didn't know these people, only Kristina, and yet they were so friendly. The food was especially good- mostly homemade- obviously these people cared a great deal about his wife and her aunt even though Shawnee had never been here before except to visit her parents' graves.

He was contrasting what he had seen and heard at the Lobo's Den to this small country church's way of greeting and caring for strangers.

Everyone seemed so friendly and eager to comfort the grieving family.

Shawnee, for her part, had cried very few tears for her aunt. She was very calm and seemed to smile a lot. Several people had hugged her for comfort and commented on how her Aunt was now at home. Shawnee seemed very much at ease here, until she glanced at her watch and it was 2:45.

She nudged Tim and whispered- "We need to be going. I've got to get to work."

He told her what he had done and she started crying. "You did that for me?!"

He nodded and they kissed. She began to cry softly. He held her close and she hugged him tightly

They stayed another ½ hour then thanked everyone for all they had done. Tim even helped clean up.

"Won't you please come to visit us?" implored Kristina.

Tim glanced at Shawnee and nodded.

Chapter 14

"Well, did you get anything more from either the funeral or the burial?"

"Nothing of use- just Frau Ludlov's history since moving here- certainly nothing we can use".

"And you are sure that the house held nothing?"

"After they sedated the dog, I had 6 full hours to search. Frau Ludlov was already dead when I got to search her room. I was in there for over 2 hours alone. Nothing".

"The trail ends here unless we find what we need."

"We still have 2 possible leads, the pharmacy girl and our deep asset."

"Until the girl meets with the McGregor woman, we probably need to monitor our deep asset non-stop- at least while they're awake."

"Shifts again?"

"Shifts my friend and hope for good luck."

"I will park the van outside the house first thing Monday morning."

Miles from Tye River church, Tim drove Shawnee toward Lovingston and home. He was about to make the turn into the aged town when she said, "Keep going."

He drove north on 29 until Covesville came into sight. The sun was not yet setting but the mountains made the day seem later than it actually was.

She directed him to Aunt Mae's house, *the lonely house, the sad little house, the house with nobody in it.*

They got out of the truck and she led him to the front porch. After a few minutes of straightening out the chain, they sat side by side on the front porch swing. It was cooling down some but the temperature was still quite pleasant.

"I don't know where to start" she began. "There are so many things that I'm confused about."

"Me too," consoled Tim.

They sat in silence for a few minutes then he said,

"One thing I know for sure. I love you and I'm sorry this has been such a terrible week for you."

She squeezed his hand and continued to be silent.

"Tomorrow is Sunday," she began slowly. "Were you serious about us visiting the Tye River Church?"

"Ah, sure. If you want. Are you certain that is where you want to go?"

"More than anything."

"Then consider it done".

She hugged him hard, smiling.

"What is going to happen to this house?" he asked.

"That's one of the projects that I have to accomplish next week. I don't know."

"What else?"

"I have to love my husband more deeply and apologize to Ingrid."

"Whoa, that first part sounds great, but apologize to Ingrid?"

"Ingrid Krause, for all her wealth and haughtiness is still a child of God. I should not be angry with her. She's just lost."

"Lost?"

"Lost. She has built her life around Dr. Jo and his earthly treasures. What do they want for? Nothing! But they are just as lost as the worst criminal. They see no need of God because wealth has blinded them."

"So why are you going to apologize to her?"

"Don't you see? She can't help doing what she does. For all her education and wealth, I can't expect them to treat me nicely- they are lost to themselves."

"Dr. Jo too?"

"Especially Dr. Jo. He should lead his house, not just in finances and business but in spiritual matters most of all. The husband is to be the head of the house. He is to be aided by his partner but if both of them don't know the path they get lost, real lost."

"But lost from what?"

"From the way, the truth and the life –Jesus".

He was listening but somewhat bothered by her description of lost people. Tim also was beginning to get convicted. He realized she was talking about the Krauses but she could just as easily have been talking about the McGregors.

" Wow, this is a lot to think about."

She nodded.

"Do you want to get something to eat?"

"I'm not really hungry but I could go for some ice cream."

He smiled- "I'll drive- Colleen –here we come!"

"One more thing Timmy. I really want to thank you for doing my job at the Lobo's Den. I just don't think I could go there tonight. By the way, what time did you get finished there?"

"It was fairly early- 4 something I think."

"4 something! You did that for me? You painted and cleaned and rescued me all in one night!" she snuggled closer to him.

He didn't realize it yet, but she was also attempting to rescue him.

They slept -in the next morning but still got up in time to actually get dressed and head to Tye River by 11:00. The small stone church was in a lovely meadow along the riverbank. Tim thought that high water might endanger the church; it was that close to the river. Tye River Church was twice the size of the Covesville church but the congregations were about equal in size.

As they entered the narthex, Tim saw for the first time his in-laws, Shawnee's parents. The Reverend and Mrs. Overton's picture hung along the passage way to the sanctuary. He looked at his bride and then closely at her mother. Her mother had been a beautiful woman.

"I see where you got your good looks!" he nudged her.

She squirmed uncomfortably and blushed. "Stop it Timmy, you know I don't like that. I'm just me".

Kristina came up excitedly and greeted them. Tim struggled with his tie, not being used to wearing anything restrictive around his neck.

Kristina and her sister, Ava, were treated just like home folks although they were probably the only Samoans for 100 miles or more. The people here continued being nice to the McGregors, proving to Tim that their care and concern was not limited to just funerals.

"We don't have a regular pastor as you know, Shawnee. We have had a series of supply pastors. Today we have a preacher from Tri-Union Theological."

"Tri-Union Theological?"

"Our deacon board is searching for the man who is called."

"*Called*- I know what that means", Tim whispered to Shawnee.

She elbowed him but grinned to herself, he's beginning to get it!

They sat down with the thirty or so others and the organist began to play.

Though organ music wasn't his favorite, he felt very much at ease.

Holy, Holy, Holy was followed by *Oh for A Thousand Tongues to Sing*. The deacon chairman welcomed the visitors and read the prayer list, asking for additions. Someone asked that the President and our troops be prayed for. A short prayer, followed by an offering led into *Onward Christian Soldiers*.

Up stood a short balding man of perhaps 30 and he was introduced as Reverend Gravely.

Tim looked at his watch as the pastor began.

"You know the church has been hijacked by politicians today" he began. "We shouldn't have to pray for our troops or our leaders, except privately. I believe it is our duty to support peace and pursue it. I believe we can best do that by not supporting this President. We need to only love one another. War is evil, and can never solve anything."

At that moment, a large, older man rose from the left front.

" Rev. Gravely, you are wrong. My sons are in the Middle East right now and I fought at Omaha Beach. A lot of men died so that you can stand there and criticize our way of life. We would not have the freedoms that we have now without someone having the guts to stop Hitler or the communists. I love peace as much as anyone but you sound like our faith should not be defended."

The short preacher was now pointing his finger at the old soldier, "You just don't understand. If we just love each other, there are plenty of nice people, good people who can bring peace to this world."

The congregation was now murmuring among themselves.

Shawnee thought – of all the preachers that Tim gets to hear, we get this guy.

The service was now in shambles. Several people apologized to the McGregors for the scene that had just occurred. No one was hostile to the Reverend Gravely, they had just heard enough.

As Tim and Shawnee headed back to the truck, Kristina called out to them, "I hope you'll come back."

Tim helped his wife into the pickup, waved and said in a tone only she could hear, "Why should we?"

"I just don't understand it. How could those nice people who helped us to much yesterday turn on that poor fellow and not let him be heard", Tim wondered aloud.

"Timmy, if the old soldier hadn't have stood up, I would have. He just beat me to it. That and the fact that we were visiting. That man was a heretic."

"Heretic? What do you mean by that?"

"Tim there is a spiritual struggle going on 24/7. One that isn't visible to the naked eye or to those who don't know Jesus".
"Go on"...
"It really requires knowing what the Bible teaches."
As they sat idling in the line of cars waiting to leave Tye River, Tim looked up and pointed.
"Does the Bible teach that?"
Shawnee watched as several of the church members shouted at Pastor Gravely and one threw something at his car. The hybrid car bearing Rev. Gravely churned across the grass parking lot and fishtailed onto the highway. The pastor gave a one-finger salute to the congregation and sped off at high speed.
"This is what going to church is all about?"
She winched as she saw all the progress he had made in the last 24 hours get washed away. She also noticed but did not tell Tim that the Reverend Gravely's car bore a rainbow flag emblem-something that the Tye River folks might not have picked up on.

Chapter 15

With November, the weather cooled considerably. They were not able to spend much day time at all together, except for part of Saturdays and all day Sunday.

The experience at Tye River had soured Tim on attending church, so despite her best wishes, they didn't.

They spent 3 Sundays in November on overnights- she working until 10 on Saturdays then they racing to some nearby overnight, only to have to get him home in time for work Mondays. It wasn't much of a relationship during the week but it gave her time to reconcile with Ingrid and to try to unravel what that week in late October had been about.

The van across from the McGregors though no longer manned, was recording their conversations around the clock. But the trail, whatever the quarry was, was now very cold. There seemed no reason to waste man hours on a stone cold trail.

Shawnee had tried to understand Ingrid. She was a fabulously wealthy woman, appealing to look at, but so lost. On the Tuesday evening, before Thanksgiving, the 2 women sat alone at the Lobo's Den, watching CNN. Another story about life decisions came on. This time, the special was about a paralyzed woman living in a trailer, who had no feeling beneath her neck. Her family was poor and unable to pay for her care adequately.

"Another one that need never have been born! A useless eater. I am tired of supporting such people," stormed Ingrid in her usual rant.

Gathering herself, Shawnee tried a different tack.

"Ingrid, who *should* be allowed to have children?"

"Only those with proper education and income and then no more than 2 children. Parents need not raise the children; the state can do a better job. Child care should be from only qualified specialists and should begin at the earliest possible age- before age 2."

"Well, I'm not sure if we are *"qualified specialists"* but I *think* Tim and I are expecting", she smiled hesitantly.

Ingrid's response could not have been any more callous.

"Oh, I hope not! I mean you are so young. What will that do to your figure? Babies steal your youth. Have you told Tim yet?"

"It was going to be part of our Thanksgiving. I want to tell him what I'm thankful for and ..."

"Do you really think you are expecting, have you run tests? How far along are you?"

"I 'm not sure but I think I could be 2½ to 3 months along, I tire easily and..."

"Please stay seated. Let me get you some tea. Here relax- you can put your feet up if you like".

Shawnee sipped the tea slowly. She closed her eyes as the music on the PA system briefly caught her attention..." *Ten years ago on a cold dark night.* I've heard that before she thought; say she was more tired, than she realized... *she walks these hills in a long black veil* ... why am I so tired???... Where's Tim???... She struggled to open her eyes but couldn't ... *nobody knows, nobody sees, nobody know but me...*

As Shawnee sank into unconsciousness, Rolf entered from the kitchen door and Ingrid hung up the CLOSED sign on the front door. Dimming the lights, they proceeded to toward the sideways escalator and then to the tram. It now being after 6:00

pm, there was no one except the staff at the infirmary that saw what happened next.

Tim was at home when the call came from the infirmary. He jumped into the truck and lit the tires all the way to the Lobo's Den. Jumping out, he forced the door open, he sped through the kitchen and entered the escalator- it was not on but he climbed it anyway. The tramline on the other side of the mountain had long ceased running so he galloped as fast as he could to the infirmary.

Once inside a Doctor Engels met him.
Trying hard to catch his breath and listen at the same time, all he heard was MISCARRIAGE and BE ALRIGHT.
He was forced to don a gown complete with mask and led into a room where his wife lay.
She lay there shallowly breathing and for many minutes, she seemed to be destined to stay asleep. He stroked her face and hair. He whispered her name and her eyes flickered.
She woke up and began to survey her surroundings. "Where..."
"Shhh.. don't try to talk... You are in good hands, you are safe..."
"What... now I remember ..."
"Shhh... It's ok, it's ok ..."
"Why are you crying?" she asked.
"Its ... well the doctor says that we will have..." he choked up heavily. In his bravest, huskiest voice, "other children". Tim was sobbing and she did her best to console him. They hugged for a very long time.

For the second time in a month, the chairman of the Tye River Church's deacon board received a phone call from Shawnee. Actually, Tim felt it was his responsibility and insisted on making the call.

They buried their daughter, Katherine Mae McGregor, without ever seeing or holding her, on Thanksgiving Day. The tiny coffin was interred next to Shawnee's parents and across from Aunt Mae. Again, the church charged nothing and there was not really a service, just a private burial.

They both wept.

This time of grief was more intense for both of them. A common loss. A heavy loss. Little in the way of comfort. The pastor from Covesville visited. Helen called. Kristina and her sister were away.

Later on Thanksgiving evening, Shawnee answered the phone. It was Reverend Inke.

"Hello, Mrs. McGregor, I understand that you have had some problems," he began.

"We have"-she said distantly.

She heard him whisper to someone-"turn that thing down"-but not before it was obvious that Rev. Inke could barely take time from the football game he was watching to call.

"Well, we have been thinking about you and hope things will improve. Take each day, one at a time, and think good thoughts. Perhaps you can visit our service again sometime."

"Perhaps."

"Well, if there is anything you need, please let Ingrid Krause know. Good-bye."

Her mind raced. *"Let Ingrid Krause know?!!"* The same Ingrid Krause who had not so much as mentioned her aunt's death? Ingrid Krause who sent not so much as a card for either funeral and expected me to work at that pagan party? Ingrid Krause, who probably rejoiced when the baby was" –she began to sob uncontrollably.

Tim held her and it took a long time to find out why the phone call had caused her such pain.

"I'm so sorry," he said.

"No, I'm sorry. I'm sorry I'm not a better person," she said through bitter tears.

"You are a wonderful, caring, loving person-what do you mean, a better person?"

"I have been hurt by several things said and unsaid. I have had my feelings hurt and I am fighting my human nature- I need to forgive those people".

"Don't you ever give in and want to just scream? "I've never really seen you angry. I get so mad sometimes that I swear- but I don't around you."

"And why is that?"

"I don't want to disappoint you".

She had stopped crying now- "That's exactly it Tim. I don't want to disappoint my best friend."

"You mean you don't want to disappoint me?"

"Of course, I don't want to disappoint you, but *YOU* didn't die for me. Jesus did. He said I should forgive those who mistreat me. You have never mistreated me" —she began to cry again— "and I love you so."

He shook his head as he held her.

For days thereafter, they both had trouble sleeping and Tim was glad that neither of them had to work. She took a sleeping pill after the 3 rd sleepless night.

He kept wondering how he could make it up to Shawnee. On Sunday morning following the burial, he awoke at 3:30, dressed and quietly prepared sandwiches.

He tip-toed past Shawnee, took their sleeping bags, a change of clothes for Shawnee, and headed toward the truck. He quickly prepared a nest for her and went in and gently lifted her and carried her to the warming truck. She barely moved as he tucked her in carefully and slowly made his way out on to Rt. 29 North.

The race was on. Could he make it to Big Meadows by sunrise?

He had heard that the view there was really beautiful. Somewhere he had heard that there was a sunrise service there each Sunday morning and maybe this could be *their sunrise*, a new beginning.

The high-powered Chevy effortlessly ate the miles and they arrived ½ hour before sunrise. He looked around carefully and decided it best to dress Shawnee himself- there wasn't really a place for her to change.

She was still somewhat groggy and it took awhile for her to understand what was happening.

He got her dressed and she was semi-awake as the first hint of dawn came from the east. It was cold outside and they snuggled in the truck, awaiting both the sunrise and the service that was to be conducted.

At about 5:45, a small group including the McGregors huddled at the outdoor overlook at Big Meadows.

A small figure moved toward the pulpit and welcomed them. The woman conducting the service began by reading:

"Oh beautiful creation, we stand in awe of what we see. The majesty of the mountains, the glory of this sunrise, help us to be good stewards of our fragile planet. We seek to preserve the marvels of nature and its intricate balance. There are those who do not understand the urgency of saving these woods and animals.

As our mother earth is regenerated even now by the streams of cascading sunlight, let us strive to be as one with nature."

From somewhere a flute began to play Koombyah and the crowd joined in haphazardly. The crowd except Shawnee –she was late for the door- she walked quickly back to the truck, climbed in and shut the door.

Tim did not understand her reaction. "What had happened? Was it more thoughts of the baby? Was the song inappropriate? Was she just an emotional basket case? Was she mad at him?" He climbed in and asked "What ..."

"It's nothing you did, Timmy. It was very sweet of you to go to all this trouble and I love you for it. Your heart is so sweet- you wanted this to be a new beginning for us and it can be..."

"But what? ... What is it this time? Another heretic?"

"Exactly. The Bible tells us that there will be a time when the creation is worshipped and not the Creator. If you listened to what she said, there was not one word about God. Mother Earth and all the plants and animals- even the sunrise- but God? No room for Him!"

He wasn't angry, just hurt and confused. Nothing he did or said seemed to please her —especially regarding her spiritual side. He had never really thought much about God-had even blamed God for his parent's death- but now it looked like although he loved his wife and she him, they were going in opposite directions.

With all these questions unanswered, they headed back to Lovingston and the new workweek. She nestled close to him and he loved that ...but there was a distance between them that he could not explain.

Chapter 16

"Absolutely not!" stormed Dr.Krause. "What possessed you to even entertain such a suggestion?"

Rolf stoically stood not blushing, but nonetheless, not appreciating the wrath of Dr. Jo. "McGregor has asked twice and..."

"You will completely disregard this request and we will have to make arrangements so that that tunnel is resealed. Make sure McGregor is not assigned to that area. We will need no further discussion of the Volkswagen in Shaft 16. Understood?"

Rolf nodded left the room.

December was unusually cold and lonely for Shawnee. Tim was gone by 4:30 am so that he could get off at the earliest possible hour but because ERWACHE was in a fast production mode, he seldom was home before 6:00 pm.

Her schedule was still Tuesday, Friday, Saturday, 4 to 10 but as the holiday season set in, it became obvious that Ingrid was going to be traveling and that Shawnee would have more responsibility. She was requested to report at 3:30 and stay until 10:30 if needed.

With Tim's hours and her extended schedule, they treasured the evenings before the fireplace and the Sundays even more.

But loneliness is all that she felt through the days of diminishing sunlight. She could go to *the sad little house, the house with nobody in it,* sit on the front porch swing and think about what might have been. Or she could play ball with Grayboy on the lawn that needed attention. Or she could try to head off the weekend chores by doing the laundry early but it seemed that when she did that, that someone was always starring at her.

On the second Wednesday of December, she decided that she would go to the Tye River church – to the graves. The graves that had doubled in just over a month. The graves that nobody else would visit- unless she took Tim with her.

At first, she thought about taking Grayboy but decided that she needed time alone. She decided to take a few small flowers and set them on each grave.

 She wanted something special for Katherine maybe a small doll or stuffed animal so, she stopped in the CVS on the way to Tye River.

"Hi, stranger! Long time no see!"- Greeted the red-haired girl behind the counter.

"Megan!" Shawnee exclaimed as she ran to hug the high school senior, who was somewhat perplexed at this outburst of emotion.

Shawnee held on to Megan with a long hug that prompted Megan to ask, "Is something wrong?"

For the first time publicly, Shawnee began to sob. Megan was even more perplexed.

For a few brief moments, Shawnee found comfort from a friend that accepted her as she was.

She began with, "I can't believe I did that. Things have just been very difficult for the last month and ½ and I just need to talk to somebody. Forgive me." Collecting herself she said," Say, it's early, why aren't you in school?"

"Combination of reasons"- Megan started- "do you see that red Mustang out there? It's an early graduation present but I have to pay for the insurance. Then there's this thing called Winter Break. With my co-op program, the teacher let us opt -out of going to school this week if we choose to work."

"Winter Break-that used to be called Christmas,"-mused Shawnee.

"Yep-back in the day. Say now, what's going on?"

"It's so complicated. I ... I don't need to trouble you with it."

"Nonsense, we're buds, right?"

Shawnee nodded.

"Well, we're going to have to have a girl to girl talk. I don't even know how the seduction worked out."

The *"seduction"* that now seemed like years ago. She smiled sadly.

"Ok, when are you off? I work Tuesday, Friday and Saturday".

"What's your tomorrow look like – in the morning?"

Shawnee said, "That would be fine- I'm up from 4:30 on so anytime..."

"4:30? You did say 4:30? Do they even have one of those in the morning?"

Shawnee smiled- "Yes, but just we old married people know about. How about 8:30?"

"Did I hear 9:00?"

"9:00 it is then- need directions?"

"Please- my Dad says I need as much direction as any one will give me".

"Ok, second Lovingston exit-take a right-go 1 block-take a right-smallest house on the block- look for the VW."

"Even I can probably find that one. I can only stay until 11:30, is that ok?"

"That is fine- now let me buy a couple of things so you don't lose your job." Shawnee scooped up some sweet rolls and some coffee.

As she was checking out at Megan's register, she said she said, "Oh, I almost forgot- ring this up too."

Megan glanced at the small doll that Shawnee placed on the counter and noticed that Shawnee clouded up again. The customer behind Shawnee, a balding man did not seem overly anxious to be checked out but still both women knew he was there.

"You sure you are alright? I can leave early today if...

"Please don't, I...I'll be ok. See you tomorrow...about 9?"
"9 it is!"

On the way to Tye River, Shawnee thanked God for putting Megan in her path.

Behind her in the parking lot, the balding man returned to his truck and spoke briefly on his cell phone- " Tomorrow- 9:00 am- we need to have the van manned- this may be the break".

Thursday morning seemed to Tim like all other days –just work and more work- in silent separation from almost every other human being. He had seen Rolf from a distance and hoped that Rolf had news about the VW in shaft 16. But Rolf had either not heard him or ignored him. Tim was sure that Rolf had seen him but dismissed it to the early hour- few things seem right at 5 am. With the VW project possibly not happening, he had stolen a few moments to work on the '32 Chevy but that was another long-term project. What could he give Shawnee for Christmas? The Company only allowed the 25th off and the 31st if someone wanted it. Still a couple of Sundays might be squeezed in- provided he could find some place to take her within the limits. All these thoughts were rolling around in his head as his wife was up and about to entertain their 2nd house guest.

Several hundred feet above and miles away, the clock approached 9. The gray van had been positioned closer to the McGregor's, now on the same side of the street. Inside sat 2 men- reviewing recent tapes.

"Just as I told you –nothing useful. Just idle chatter and talk to the dog."

"If this day yields nothing, we may have to break in and look for ourselves."

"By whose authority? We have even less "authority" than we had at Frau Ludlov's".

"My friend we do not have endless time or resources- something has to come up today or the trail may end, here".

Megan was, surprisingly for her, on time. Shawnee welcomed her into the small house and they chatted briefly for a few moments about light things- school, the new Mustang, CVS.

Then Megan said- "Ok, what gives? What's happening in your life that has you so upset?"

Shawnee picked up Aunt Mae's book and said, "I guess it all started with this book. Remember this picture?"

"Sure".

Shawnee recounted the abbreviated trip to Peaks of Otter, her aunt's death, the "Halloween" party..."

At that point, Megan interrupted- "Oh, yeah, even we heard it got pretty wild. There were some kids from school whose parents went and...."

"I knew it, I knew I wasn't wrong...Then there was the miscarriage..."-at which point she broke down again.

Megan tried to comfort her friend but Shawnee was more composed today than she had been the day before.

Shawnee excused herself and when she came back in, she had Grayboy with her.

He was excited to see Megan but more pleased to be inside since it was cold outside.

"So you say everything started with this book?" Megan asked as she looked at he faded blue book. She opened the book- "This is really pretty handwriting- wonder what language it is?"

Out on the street, in the cold gray van, the 2 men listening were beside themselves.

Shawnee said- "I don't know- maybe German- I plan on getting it translated once I find someone I trust to do it."

"Well, I don't know anyone who can help, but as far as all this other stuff that has happened to you-well my Dad says that stuff just happens- except that he uses worse language. I guess you will just have to be tough and hope things get better. You have your own house and if the pictures do him any justice, a hunk for husband-things can't be but so bad. I mean- sure, you've had it rough but you just have to pick yourself up and keep going. You can do it. You know maybe you and Tim could help chaperone our Senior Class trip- it would keep your mind off of your troubles and I'm sure you'd have fun."

Shawnee nodded and then realized that Megan had done her best-

The friends parted and Shawnee decided she needed some air- she said to Grayboy-"Bring your ball. Let's go up to the courthouse lawn."

This was a 3-block walk that they sometimes took, that they both enjoyed. She was pensive as they walked. No one seemed to see things as she saw them. Her sense of loneliness seemed now more acute. She was grateful for the interest shown to her by the dog- he accepted her as she was. Good ol' Grayboy..

As soon as they were out of sight- from the gray van, two well-dressed men emerged, who promptly headed to the rear door of the McGregor's home. The small house soon yielded the faded blue book that Megan had referred to. As one of the men furiously photographed the books' contents, the other man, still with a listening device attached to his ear, said, "Take your time- they are playing fetch."

Shawnee returned to the house and put Grayboy out back. He seemed more agitated than usual. "Now take it easy on the squirrels Grayboy," she cautioned. "They are just getting set up for the winter."

She looked around the small home and wondered what to do. Megan hadn't been much help but at least she listened –sorta. It was Thursday, just after 1:30. It was getting colder and the radio said that snow might be coming. She looked around and decided to go back to Tye River- she felt somehow drawn there, even though she had spent time there just yesterday.

She drove slowly toward the stone church and noticed that the same dark blue minivan was there today as was yesterday.

It began to lightly snow-as she knelt, praying at the grave of her daughter...

"Little daughter, I love you... it's snowing... I wish you could be here..."she struggled. "I know by now you have met your Grandparents and Aunt Mae- oh, how I miss you all. It's so cold and lonely here now- but I know you are all with Jesus and someday we will all be together. I just miss you so..." she was sobbing.

Gradually, though, she realized that she was not alone. There were two people standing next to her, each with a hand on her shoulder. She did not know how long they had been there but as she looked up, she saw a young man and a young woman in prayer.

Shawnee started to rise, but slowly eased back to her knees. The couple each kissed her on the side of her head and helped her to get up.

"We are so sorry to intrude," the man said quietly. "Let me introduce myself- I'm Don Trumbel and this is my wife Martha. We saw you here yesterday and last week as well. "

"We have been "trying out" for this church for the last 3 weeks- so please forgive us if we intruded on your time of grief. We hoped that we might provide some comfort," said the tall lady, Pastor Trumbel's wife.

Shawnee stood in amazement- first at the size of the couple- Shawnee was 5'8". Martha had to be every bit of 6' and Pastor Don towered over her. Her Tim was 6'4" but she guessed the Pastor to be 6'5" at the least.

"Oh, thank you- no please – I appreciate your support"... Shawnee managed to say.

The trio headed toward the church as the snow picked up in intensity.

On the inside, Shawnee's first impression of the Trumbel's proved to be correct. They were young, not much older than she and they were a *big* couple.

Pastor Don had played football at Liberty University in Lynchburg. He had been an All- Big South linebacker and second team All –American. While at Liberty he had met and been drawn to Martha Kusic, Liberty's tall and slender, All-

Big South soccer mid-fielder and First team All American, a fact that she often teased Pastor Don about. They had married and she had worked while he made his way through seminary.

They spent the next 2 hours getting acquainted and sharing their biographies. Martha related their wedding day and how it was memorable for a reason that few people would ever hear about.

"Just as the pastor was about to pronounce us man and wife," she said gazing at Don Trumbel, "my Don turned to the congregation and said, 'All this marriage and life together stuff is important but more important is that Martha and I know that we have eternal life through Jesus Christ - not because we are good people or that we have done anything to deserve eternal life. Jesus said that there is no way to go to the father except through Him. Is there any one here in this congregation that does not know Jesus as Savior? Please come forward and let us help you settle your eternal destination.' Do you know 5 people got saved at our wedding?!"

Shawnee quietly reflected on her own wedding. Only 7 people had been there, how many were saved? (the pastor, the organist, she and Aunt Mae)

Pastor Don was especially intrigued about the fact that he might soon be using the same pulpit that Shawnee's father had used, all those years ago.

It was now nearing 5 pm and the snow had not yet let up. They looked at the blanket of white covering their cars and the grave-yard.

"It's so cold... my little girl..-Her voice trailed off..

"Remember, Shawnee, she's not here- she is risen- just as He promised," said Martha.

"At least you and Tim were going to have her. So many in our culture abort out of nothing but convenience," the pastor added.

"While he was alive, Don and I worked with Reggie White and his wife to bring the abortion issue to public attention."

"Who was Reggie White?"

Pastor Don took over- "He was perhaps the greatest football lineman to ever play the game. He was also a very committed Christian. He decided to let his faith be shown to everyone he met."

"The media didn't like that," Martha added, "but the Whites let the public hear how evil the abortion industry is."

"Industry?"

"We taught anyone who would listen, that soon babies would not only be killed for convenience sake but maybe even for, "spare parts", the Pastor continued. "There has been a virtual news blackout about what is involved in an abortion. Especially partial birth abortion- where they allow the baby to be born feet first and then before the head is delivered the brains are sucked out."

She thought deeply about an event in her early life. When she and her parents went to Washington, D.C., in 1990, for the National Right to-Life Rally on the Lincoln Memorial grounds. She was 6 or 7 years old but remembered her parents talking about it for years thereafter. It was a very hot day. There were by many estimates that placed between 2 and 8 hundred thousand people there. The story was "spiked" by the media. That same week her father had seen a 2-minute headline story on the 800 gay activists that "flooded the streets of Washington". These long dormant memories still had her grappling to understand the news and who interpreted it.

Shawnee paled.

Martha noticed this change in Shawnee and said –"Don, we need to let Shawnee get home. The snow is getting deeper and she may have trouble..."

"Oh, course- forgive me. Let's let you go with a word of prayer,

Dear Lord we thank you for this young grieving mother, the love she has shown for her child and for her husband. We ask that you keep her safe on her way home. Thank you for allowing us this time together, In Jesus' name, we thank you."

They hugged her good —bye and invited her to come back anytime. "The church is voting on us the Sunday before Christmas. Some of their main, old-line families are traveling now. So we'll know soon."

"Are you sure you don't want us to drive you home?" asked Martha. "How's that bug do in the snow?"

"I'll be fine. Thank you both."

And thank you, JESUS she thought to herself as she paced the beetle slowly home.

Chapter 17

As the days before Christmas drew nearer, she decided that since the Lobo's Den was her assignment, then she would do her best to at least make it festive. She had been told that Ingrid was out of the country and would not return until after the first of the New Year.

With all good intentions, she began to spruce up the "Den", complete with flashing lights and a Christmas tree. Tim was recruited to bring one in on the Friday night before Christmas. He wasn't much at decorations but he was glad to help if that made her load lighter.

On the Saturday, before Christmas, there was less traffic than usual and Shawnee considered closing the shop down. Suddenly, Dr. Jo entered and began to berate her.

"What are all these decorations for? Who authorized this? Take them down immediately. When you have finished, see me. I will be in the office."

She was crushed. Here she had done what she thought she should do to possibly attract business and it was all wrong. She knew that she could not take the tree down by herself so she undecorated it and figured that Tim could help later.

With great hesitation, she reported to the Den's office. There, Dr. Jo, now quite drunk, ogled her.

"Sit down you sweet thing," he drooled. "You have been working here for awhile now- you know that all changes must be approved- my wife is not here for the next 2 weeks- you will ask me if anything is to change-understood?"

She nodded.

"And how is the newlywed couple- happy and satisfied with each other or do you find yourself seeking more from life? You really are quite lovely." -he breathed on her and the stench of alcohol was overwhelming. "You know, even those of us at the top-sometimes get lonely- especially this time of the year- if you find yourself lonely sometime – you can call..."

" Shawnee ? " Never had she found Tim's voice more welcome. "In here." She met him at the door and explained that the tree now needed to be removed-

"Dr. Krause, is that all that you need us to do tonight- it's 9:00- and I thought that we might as well close- since no one..."

"Yes, yes, of course. Perhaps next week will be better for business."

"Timmy –do I ever owe you!" she declared as she hurried them out on to the porch.

"What do you owe me?"

"You rescued me again from ..."

"Dr. Jo.? He's harmless- he wouldn't hurt ..."

"Now listen to me Tim McGregor- another 2 minutes and I think he would have attacked me!"

Tim did not know what to make of any of this. Here was the man who had "rescued" him from a life in an institution, a man who had hired and promoted him in ERWACHE. A man who had always treated him fairly-now the same man was coming on to his wife? Where was the sense in any of this? He couldn't have his wife afraid of the owner of the company- but he also knew that Dr.Jo would either not remember or blame the alcohol- so perhaps the best action was no action.

"I promise I'll look into it," he said, not knowing how or when he could fulfill his promise.

"So what would you like to for this Sunday?" he asked. "I think if we are real sneaky, we can slip across the Potomac and see the National Christmas tree in Washington, D.C., if you want."

"Oh that's really sweet of you..."

"But..."

"Well, Timmy," she purred, "I was really hoping that we might go back to Tye River tomorrow."

He swallowed hard and rolled his eyes. "What's on the bill this time – fist fights? Texas death match? Chain saws from 20 paces?"

She giggled and pinched his side. "Now, c'mon, Timmy. I feel like this time is going to be just right, one more time just for me?"

He melted as she gave him *that* look. He just could not resist *that* look.

Meanwhile, on the other side of the Potomac, a phone call was just concluding.

"I'm sorry to report that all of our translators are on holiday. January 29th looks like the first available appointment. Will that be sufficient?"

No –shook the head of the man listening on the other line.

" That will be fine," contradicted the man on the main line. "Please contact us here at this number when your best translator returns, thank you." He hung up.

"We can't wait until the 29th."

"I know that, but what if we can't find a Lithuanian translator before then- at least we will ultimately get the book translated."

"I just hope our quarry doesn't feel us closing in."

"I *also* hope we can spring before we are discovered."

Sunday morning before Christmas was white- at least in the Virginia Mountains. A total of 6 inches of snow covered everything. With the fireplace roaring and snow falling, Tim did not want to budge. What more could a guy ask for. The snow, the fire, the girl, even the dog. This was heaven or at least what he envisioned heaven to be like. His thoughts were interrupted by the figure of his wife leaning over him and whispering, "Timbo, time to rise and shine- it's almost 10."

Almost ten, let's see, that means cuddle up with Shawnee for another 2 hours and then it would the NFL pre-game show...

At that precise instant, he felt himself being uncovered, slowly. The series of tugs and the cheerleading from Shawnee, told him that he was being double-teamed and that Grayboy was her willing accomplice. She was laughing and he was smiling too by the time Grayboy finished.

They showered, dressed, took one last look at that comforting fire and headed for the door. Grayboy, successfully having pled his case, got to stay inside.

The Chevy fired right up and just for general principles; he dropped it down into 4-wheel drive. The old truck navigated the snowy roads without hesitation.

"Well, at least if there is a fight today, we can get out of there," Tim chided.

She punched his side and they laughed.

The Tye River church was perhaps 2/3 full when they got there. They were greeted by Kristina-"So good to see you again," she hugged Shawnee as Tim said, "Well, we said we'd be back."

Shawnee shot him a look that froze his words. He looked skyward and smiled.

Shawnee introduced Tim to Pastor Don and Martha. She had guessed correctly. The pastor was slightly taller than Tim and outweighed him by a good 40-50 pounds.

Tim quietly asked Shawnee- "Are they today's targets?"

She rammed her elbow squarely into his side. They made their way into the middle section of the pews, sat, and reviewed the church bulletin.

It was about 10:45 and everyone seemed to be awaiting the arrival of someone special. Actually, some ones .The Russell/

Davenport family were by most reckonings, the power brokers of the church. Their family roots stretched back to before there was a Tye River church- back to the days after the Civil War, after the valley had been destroyed by Union General Sheridan. The Russells and Davenports had donated the land and labor to build the church.

At 10:56, they showed themselves in and headed toward the middle section of pews, right toward Tim and Shawnee.

A very obnoxious loud woman of about 60 almost shouted at Tim, "You are in our seats!"

He and Shawnee beat a hasty retreat as the other 18 members of the clan took up the middle section.

Kristina leaned forward toward Shawnee-and whispered loud enough for Tim to hear- "My sister and I have been coming here regularly for 3 years. We've never seen some of those people."

Shawnee nodded and Tim's *'I told you so '* expression won him no points from his wife.

The service was beginning. The organist played several Christmas carols that everyone was familiar with. In between the offering and the prayer concerns, Martha Trumbel sang beautifully, *What Child Is This?*

Tim squeezed Shawnee's hand as he thought of the baby.

Pastor Trumbel's message was simple- Yes we celebrate the birth of the baby Jesus but that baby grew up and became the only way that all people have to reach God. While we celebrate the birth, we should also worship Him for dying for us. He, who knew no sin, became sin for whosoever will come to Him. He gave an invitation to accept Jesus as savior, saying that no better decision could be made at this time of year.

As the organist played *Just As I Am,* Tim felt his throat tighten. He began to sweat and did not want to look at Shawnee.

2 people went forward and accepted Jesus.

"That's 2 more than we've seen in 3 years," –whispered Kristina.

The service ended and the congregation remained seated. The Trumbel's were escorted into the pastor's study and the chairman of the deacon board entertained a motion to discuss calling Pastor Don.

"Here we go," said Tim ducking lower into his seat.

"Too strident. Much too strident!" crowed the matriarch of the Davenport entourage.

"I agree entirely," said the elder Russell, who looked very much like his wife's puppet.

"Let's all be reasonable. We're good country people here. We like to have fun and well, church shouldn't be so...so"

"Religious?"

"Yes, religious. You know that many of my family are in the Masonic. My uncle is a 32nd degree Mason. He's a good man- but the Mason's are more..."

"Inclusive," finished still another member of *the* family. "The Masonic and Eastern Star believe in the universal brotherhood of man. All religions should be acknowledged."

"Why, I think that this pastor and his wife probably don't have room for all the grand old songs of the season- *Jingle Bells, White Christmas,, Silver Bells*, why they probably don't even believe in Santa Claus."

Up to this point, Shawnee had been barely able to sit still. Santa, was the last straw.

"May I speak?" she said rising. Tim sunk lower still.

"And who might you be Miss?" asked one of *the family.*

"Well, technically I'm not a member here but I am a Christian and my father was pastor here..."

"Let her speak! was challenged by "she's not one of us!"

Shawnee took the pulpit and the crowd grew silent.

"I am Shawnee McGregor. I work at the Espresso Bar at Lovingston. I am no one special. 4 of my family are buried out in the graveyard here. This church has a simple decision to make- is it here to be like the world or save people from the world. I have only just met the Trumbels but I know they love Jesus and believe that life is too short to serve in a church that does not want to spread the good news of Jesus Christ. So what will it be, Tye River? The World, the flesh and the devil or Jesus the Savior of man?"

She did not get an answer to her question- she saw Tim slip out the side door and head for the truck.

She excused herself and followed her husband through the snow.

This time it was Shawnee who was confused.

"Tim, what's wrong?"

"I ...I don't really know- I don't like you being criticized and yet I don't know enough to defend you- we, I just don't see this church stuff- why is it so important- I mean we do ok —we love each other.."

She nodded.

"I just don't know what to do or say- can we just go home and talk?"- He asked.

"Sure, I don't need to go back in there- I ... I should have kept quiet..."

"I don't think you should have." Tim countered, surprising her. "You obviously care a great deal about other people's lives ..."

"It's not just their lives; it's their souls, their eternity..."

"See all that is important but I don't know enough and anyway how can you or anybody be sure you have it all right? Some of those arguments that came up- the Eastern Star and all, how do you know what you believe is right?"

Shawnee knew there was no quick way to teach Tim what she believed. If he wanted to know —it was her job to nudge him along.

"Ok, for now, let's just say that I know what I believe. We all have to make choices- I chose Jesus."

He started the truck and silence inundated the cab- neither one wanting to say anything further. Absently, he switched on the radio- his favorite country station announced-"And here is George Jones,"

I've had choices since the day that I was born,
There were voices that told me right from wrong,
If I had listened, I wouldn't be here today,
Living and dying with the choices I've made...

She thought – thank you God for using that song.
He thought – wow, how coincidental is that?

Christmas morning he awoke early and hoped to surprise her with breakfast in bed. She was already up and cooking. He made some excuse about checking something in the backyard but wouldn't let Grayboy investigate. She grew suspicious but absolutely wilted as Tim presented her with a box- a box that moved on it's own.

She opened it to find 2 yellow kittens- she was so excited that she burned the grits-again!

She gave him some of his presents- a new shotgun, a 4-man tent- and a Bible.

He looked at her with awe- "I've never had a Bible of my own-thank you" he said, though she noticed he seemed more interested in the tent and shotgun. She got him both of Charlie Daniels break- through CDs *The Door* and *Steel Witness*, and some other Southern Gospel favorites. She was trusting that Charlie Daniels could help Tim get to *"the"* Door.

For his part, Tim had bought her a few things- some clothes, a CD player and some country music CDs.

He said, "I was hoping to upgrade your ride-maybe later."

"Oh Tim, this is the biggest Christmas I've ever had! As an MK, we used to get 2 or 3 gifts. Thank you for loving me and for all these presents. I have 1 more for you."

She handed him an envelope, which he nervously opened.

"Wow- 2 nights and 2 days at the hotel of my choice at Virginia Beach- how neat! Oh, thank you"- he kissed her, and began the last phase of *his* surprise.

"I almost forgot- could you please get the envelop from under Grayboy's bed?"

Puzzled she walked over toward Grayboy who was warily watching the *"yellow peril"* that was inching its way toward him. He seemed appreciative of Shawnee's attention if only momentarily, as the 2 intruders came ever closer. Shawnee grabbed the envelope and scooped up the kittens- hugging them and making a fuss over them.

She sat, handed the kittens to Tim and opened the envelope.

Inside was a statement from the law firm of Tuttle and Bauserman. She read through it and asked, "Does this mean what I think it means?"

He nodded.

"You can't be serious! Tim... I..."

"Don't know what to say?"

She began to tear up and then ran to his side.

"How?"

"Even if I have to sell the truck, I do have $18,000 in just the engine- I'm going to buy you Mae's house. I've got them researching it. "

Their Christmas day ended and it was back to work the next morning for Tim. She had 2 days to get into a rhythm before she was to go back to work.

The kittens took some getting used to. Grayboy suddenly liked going outside, even in the coldest weather. He also had to yield his bed to 2 disrespectful kittens that snatched his spot next to the fire while he felt sorry for himself outside.

Tim often wondered if he had been sane when he bought not 1 but 2 of these noisemakers. He took to calling them, Dumb and Dumber.

Shawnee chided him- "They are just babies. Babies have to be taught."

"Don't babies have to be teachable?"

She smiled, "They are so sweet, just like their Daddy."

"Well, what are you going to call them – 2 cats in search of a brain?"

She poked him and announced, "Goodness and Mercy."

"Goodness and Mercy?"

"Yep. *When* you start reading your Bible, there is a verse that says

"'Surely Goodness and Mercy shall follow me all the days of my life'... Since you brought them in here Christmas morning, they follow me everywhere. They even tried to come in the shower."

For the record, New Year's Eve was an optional day off and the McGregors took the day and talked about their future. She was so excited about the prospect of owning Aunt Mae's house that that is all she talked about. For his part, Tim seemed to have finally *"hit a home run"* as far as pleasing Shawnee. He was pleased she was pleased and for now things looked really good. In truth, the law firm had its work cut out for them, Mae having left no will. It might mean, Tim was told, that the state of Virginia could end up with the house. With that in mind, he suggested that they search the house for a will to see if one existed.

Thus on New Year's Eve, the 5 of them, Tim, Shawnee, Grayboy and the yellow terrorists, Goodness and Mercy, inspected Mae's house. Sadly, they found very little to go on. Mae had drawers full of receipts but nothing that conveyed her wishes once she passed on.

As they explored, Shawnee from time to time would say, "And this room will be blue, we need green accents here..., the mantle will need to be refinished ..."

Tim never tired of her vision and her enthusiasm. The same could not be said for Grayboy who found Goodness and Mercy in hot pursuit at every turn.

Toward evening Tim said, "You know it's really sad, this lady lived here for all this time, yet she really didn't have very much. Some old furniture, a few books, she was really quite poor. She probably hadn't had anything new for 50 years."

"She didn't put value on things, Timmy. She probably hadn't had much new or nice by our standards- but if she had, say a new car or a new coat, she couldn't take that with her, could she?"

He seemed set back at that thought.

"She didn't have a lot of treasure here but I treasure the brief time I knew her and I'm richer for having known and loved her."

Their philosophical discussion ended when Grayboy rounded the corner and slid behind them as the *yellow menace* bounded in.

They drove home, somewhat dejected at not having found a will but at least heartened by the time spent in the house. Despite the neglect forced on it by Mae's old age, the house was really in pretty solid shape.

Once they got home, they started the fire and sat before it, trying to figure out a timetable for the New Year.

ERWACHE 's holiday schedule was different than most every other company that the McGregors had ever heard of.

"Let's see", she began putting a fresh piece of paper over the old faded blue book. "Besides Sundays and the usual, Thanksgiving and the recent holidays, this year, we have January 20th, March 7th, March 16th, April 20th, May 1st, July 4th, September 9th, 14th, 28th, October 7th, 29th and 31st. We should get a big calendar to mark down our goals," she exclaimed.

"Say I saw a nifty one at the CVS..."

"I saw that same one and no I don't think that will do- You'd think that those girls would have found their clothes by now" –she mock frowned, but in reality she was disappointed that he still was looking at things like that.

"Oh, and don't forget we can get a week's vacation once you finish your first year"- he proclaimed.

That sounded so much like a sentence-she really was not looking forward to the Lobo's Den at all.

"Say, don't forget about the 2 days at Virginia Beach- this could be a really busy year."

Neither of them had any idea of how their lives would change in just the first few weeks of the New Year. As she set the new list of things to do inside the old blue book, suddenly it hit her.

"Timmy, what if Mae's will is in this book, in a language we can't read!"

They looked at each other-smiling then laughing like 2 giddy children.

Tim offered, "I bet the Krauses can help translate it!"
She froze at the thought. "I'm not sure we..."
"Don't worry. I'll talk Dr. Krause tomorrow."

Out on the snowy street, the unmanned van continued to monitor the McGregor's conversation. The news that the Krauses were to be involved with the translation of the old book shook the nerves of the spies, when finally they checked the tapes.

True to his word, the next evening, Tim presented the old faded blue book to Dr. Jo.
"And where did you come by this?" asked the ERWACHE founder, coyly.
"It belonged to Shawnee's Aunt Mae- you may remember her from the wedding- she was wheel chair bound and..."
"Yes of course, that pitiful creature in the wheelchair... how is she?"
"She died just before Halloween."
"Hmmmph... pity- I don't read Polish, that is what I believe it to be, but I have a friend at UVA who may be able to help. It appears to a book of fantasy based on the few words I know- I will see that my friend gets to it shortly. What else do you require?"
Needing nothing else, he was dismissed and headed home.

Later that night, ERWACHE's board met in executive session.
"Let this be a warning to everyone. The mere existence of this book means that someone, seeking to destroy all that we have built, could go to the authorities and begin investigating us. This book will be accidentally lost, the McGregors will be consoled for the loss, but we must be more vigilant."
"Sir, they like all of our employees are monitored- shall we do a 24/7 micro study?"
"Not yet, they are too pedestrian to know much- if they act suspiciously then, yes. Gentlemen, that old skeleton had our

historic work minutely detailed. This was a very close call-I have made a photocopy of the contents which I shall put in the company safe.

As for Frau Ludlov and her book- good riddance," he said tossing the old book into the blazing fireplace. In a few minutes, Aunt Mae's entire book was ash.

Chapter 18

Their reunion was frigid at best. Ingrid returned to the Lobo's Den, looking years younger, tanned, rested, but with a strutting arrogance that was difficult to endure. Based on all the tension that Shawnee felt, this was a time for just business.

"I see that the store did not prosper in my absence. To what do you attribute this failure?"

"Well, I tried to decorate the shop as festively as I..."

"Oh, yes. Josef mentioned something about unflattering seasonal tripe. What possessed you to do such a thing?"

"I'm sorry I thought that by having some Christmas decorations up that..."

"That will be quite enough about Christmas- let us return to the situation at hand- we need business- we are going to maintain the store as is BUT we will have open house every Saturday displaying local artists and their works in the upstairs galleries. Our hours will remain the same but your duties will be on both floors. Understood?"

Shawnee nodded and said, "I need to mention that you had several calls from EXACTICHIP- they said it was very important that you contact them as soon..."

"Fine, thank you – we need not discuss this matter again..."

With that, she turned and walked away.

Fighting temptation for all she was worth, Shawnee gave in and stuck her tongue out at Ingrid. Shawnee immediately blushed and felt guilty but somewhat relieved as well.

"'Unflattering seasonal tripe!' that's what she called it." Shawnee steamed later that night. "I'm trying hard not to say something- but if anyone ever was on a high horse its Ingrid. Tim, I just don't know if I can continue working with that woman."
"I'm sure it's tough but if we can stay on the same work schedule and vacation schedule, that will help us in getting the house fixed up. Plus the money is great and that house will need lots- please see if you can hang on, I promise I'll take you more places. OK?"
"We'll see. No promises —not yet- there are still some things that I'd like to have explained."
"Like?"
"Like- how can I work with someone who didn't even acknowledge the 2 deaths we suffered? Like how did she find us when we went to Peaks of Otter- like why does she not like people having children unless it's the *right people*. How about those for starters?"
Tim, holding her close, said, "I don't know those answers but I am hoping that all this won't matter once we move to Mae's".
"That is 'if' we move to Mae's. Have you heard anything from Dr.Jo?"
"I have an appointment with him tomorrow after work. The Krauses will be gone from January 19-21, so I'd hope to have some news before they go."

That same evening at Castle Krause, Dr. Jo and Ingrid were immersed in their hot tub- discussing the McGregors.
"Neither is overly smart. I'm certain no copies of the book were made except the one in the vault."
"I do not trust the woman. There is something in her spirit that unsettles me. She is an adequate worker but she seems to be constantly looking around. Perhaps when you tell Timothy that the book was meaningless drivel, you might insure that they

will not suspect anything by telling them about the house- that they were to receive it – that bone might keep them quiet and less restive."

"An idea well conceived, my dear. We can insure their compliance with our wishes and keep them well distracted by restoring the house of that vermin Ludlov."

"I have read what that hag wrote- we must be sure that no one ever sees the copy you made."

At 6:15 pm, the next evening, Tim met with Dr. Jo at the zeppelin port.

"Tim, I'm afraid I have both good and bad news- the bad first- your book –or that of your wife's has been lost- my friend took it with him on a skiing holiday and lost it. I am quite sorry. The good news is that he read the book in its entirety and as I suspected it was a book of fantasy and make believe. However, written at the end was a short passage about your wife, Barbara, that..."

"Shawnee, My wife Shawnee."

"Of course. Her aunt wrote that when she died, she would leave the house to Sharon."

"Shawnee? Did you mean Shawnee?"

"What – oh yes, yes, of course."

"But without the book for proof, how can we claim that the will even existed?"

Coldly, with exact precision, Dr.Jo said-"There will be no problems- everything will be arranged for you. You may go."

Tim, as he turned to go, considered asking one more question- but the founder of ERWACHE had walked hurriedly away.

Tim was floored. The house would be theirs'. He hurried home to tell Shawnee.

He was surprised to find her on the phone when he got home. They did not have many friends, and the phone seldom rang.

He patted Grayboy and even paid 30 seconds of attention to Goodness and Mercy, who now seemed preoccupied by Grayboy's tail.

Shawnee motioned to him to wash up and that she had dinner ready.

He heard her say, "That is really good news- I'd love to come- I don't know if Tim will be joining me. Next Wednesday night then, 7:00 pm. Thank you for thinking of us." She hung up and gave Tim a big hug.

"Who was that?" he asked.

"That was Kristina, from Tye River. They are going to have a Bible study each Wednesday night and we are invited!"

"Oh," said Tim.

"Would you go with me? The Trumbels will be leading it."

"So they got confirmed or whatever?"

"Kristina said it was a very close vote and that several families left the church including several *"pillars"*. But the Trumbels have been accepted by the community since then and they are going to be having Bible study each week. So how about it, is it a date?"

"I don't know, something else has come up- something I think is more important."

She gave him a quick look- "What could be more important than a date with your wife?"

"Nothing is more important than a date with my wife", he affirmed, "but I think we are both going to be very busy from now on. Dr.Jo said that the house is ours!"

"What...how...?"

"The man who was translating the book said that at the end- the last entry probably before she had her stroke, Aunt Mae gave you the house!"

"Oh, that's what I had dreamed would happen. I have prayed that God would provide a way for us to get it. God is so good!""

Tim hugged her. They stood still for a long time-just hugging.

"What else did the book say?"

"Just some writings about her life –nothing notable."

"Can we get the translation and the book back - I'd like to read it and take it to the Bible study as an answer to prayer?"

"Well, the bad news is that the book has been misplaced but ..."

"Misplaced? Misplaced how? Where is it?"

"Well apparently the man, who was translating, took it on a ski vacation and left it wherever he was. But according to Dr. Jo, his friend said that the house is yours."

"<u>*Ours,*</u>" she corrected- "but what else did the book say? I know so little about my aunt- can the man who translated the book send us a copy- I really can't believe the book is gone."

"I didn't ask about that but I will see if we can get a copy for you- I asked Dr.Jo how we could prove ownership without a will."

"And what did he say?"

"He said everything would be taken care of, then he dismissed me."

"Dismissed?"

"He decided the conversation was over".

"That's the way that Ingrid is too. Do you think that everything is going to work out?"

"I guess so. Anyway, we need to get started on our plans so every evening that we have, we need to devote to getting started."

"Well, I don't want to sound ungrateful, because I am really excited, and I want to thank you for going the extra mile and getting the book translated..."

"*But*"- here it comes, another of the famous buts, he thought to himself

"But we need a firm foundation if we are going to work on this house- The Bible says:

"*Unless the Lord builds the house, they that labor, labor in vain.*"

"Translation?"

"We need to go to the Bible study to build *our* relationship with God."

"You said *our*, you really meant *my* relationship, didn't you?"

"Tim we both need Him- won't you please come with me?"

"Look, that's a whole week from now, let me think about it, ok?

"Fair enough. How about church this Sunday?"

His look was enough for her not to press any further.

3 days later when the McGregor's conversation was finally reviewed, the men waiting for the Lithuanian translator to return, were highly agitated.

Their photocopy of Mae's book was all that probably remained of the evidence that they sought- they could afford no mistakes or years of investigation might forever be lost. An accurate translation was vital.

On Friday, Shawnee reported for work just, before 4:00 pm.

The Lobo's Den was a beehive of activity. All morning, members of the local wine growing community had been moving samples and displays into the overly large attic. It was apparent that several of those involved in the move had been sampling each other's wines-, as several were *quite friendly* –much to her dismay.

Once the dinner hour arrived, there were fewer people as the locals had been preparing for the big event tomorrow- a Free Wine Tasting and Art Display. Visions of the horrors of October 31 were racing through her head when she looked up to see a very handsome man sit down at the Espresso bar. It was just now 7:30. The man was deeply tanned and very blond. His emerald green eyes were almost as intense as Shawnee's.

"You have the most beautiful green eyes," he said, causing her to blush instantly. "You are perhaps the loveliest girl I have ever seen."

Not knowing how to respond, she said nothing.

"I am George Waters Panch. My friend's call me GW. Please consider me your friend- 'cause I'd sure like to be yours." He extended his hand and she weakly shook it.

He continued- "I understand that there is to be an open house and art display here tomorrow. I parked my Rodeo out on the street, will it be ok there? "

She nodded.

"My dear girl, are you able to speak? If not, you are still the most beautiful girl I've ever seen."

Fighting back her modesty, she finally said, "I'm sorry, you... just caught me off guard, I'm not used to people being so nice to...I mean..." she was now quite flustered and her voice trailed off. She regrouped her thoughts and finally managed, "What part do you play in this open house tomorrow?"

"I'm a model. Say has anyone ever painted you?"

She blushed again.

"Well I know some pretty good painters and you would be well paid- the work is easy and you –well you arc just so lovely!"

At that instant, Ingrid mercifully interrupted. Never had Shawnee welcomed her boss's presence before.

Ingrid spirited GW away and Shawnee was so grateful when her Tim walked in at 9:00. She clung to him, glad that Ingrid and GW never reappeared.

As she shut the doors of the Den, the music overhead played a familiar yet strange song:

"She walks these hills in a long black veil..."

She thought –why does that song trouble me so?"

On the way home, she said, "I just don't know Tim. Can't I please try to get another job-somewhere?"

She replayed the evenings' conversations and what she was facing tomorrow. Tim decided to stay close to her tomorrow-especially since she was so upset by just one man's confirmation of what Tim already knew- she was the most beautiful girl in the world. Tim wanted to be there to protect her.

Saturday morning dawned cold and snowy.

"Good" she thought- "the snow will keep the crowd down."

They had the usual chores to do on Saturday but as the clock neared the 4 pm hour, the butterflies in her stomach got bigger. She became even more anxious when she saw the large number of cars and trucks that lined the street outside the Lobo's Den. GW's Rodeo apparently had not moved all night –since it was covered in snow. Evidently, the Den had been open for quite some time.

She was so glad Tim walked her in, and then sat down at the Espresso bar. The first hour passed relatively without event. There was very little traffic downstairs but it was obvious from the sound of multiple footsteps that there was quite a gathering upstairs.

Tim was reading a hunting magazine and listening to the live band that this week was playing classical music. The snow continued to fall.

Ingrid breezed down the stairs and not seeing Tim, said sharply to Shawnee- "Where have you been?" We need you to serve the guests upstairs- go to the kitchen and get the hors d'oeuvres. *NOW!*"

Suddenly, Tim entered her view and she smiled a crooked smile.

As she emerged from the kitchen, she glanced at Tim and he winked and gave her a thumbs up.

She winched and made her way up the staircase, passing a pair of men who were holding hands.

Tim's eyes traveled across the ceiling as he envisioned her walking from guest to guest in the attic.

Suddenly a loud crash interrupted the classical quartet on stage and the congregation in the attic. Tim interpreted it to be the tray that Shawnee was carrying-so he thought he had better investigate.

He ran into his wife –now ashen pale –as she passed him on her way down stairs. She did not stop but headed straight for the kitchen.

He decided that she had simply dropped the tray and that she would probably take care of it. He waited for her to emerge from the kitchen but when she did not, he decided to investigate. He found her cowering in the corner near the sink-apparently having just thrown up.

"Shawnee, are you sick?"

All she could do was point toward the upstairs. He approached her and she just as adamantly pointed to the upstairs.

Reluctantly, he headed upstairs –even Tim was not ready for what he saw.

There were perhaps a 20 artists-each with their own easel, busily painting 2 naked men who were engaged in a sex act that had been illegal in most civilized nations prior to the 1990's.

Tim was shocked at the sight but even more unprepared for Ingrid's words as she brushed up against Tim.

"I didn't know you were interested in art Timothy. Isn't that tall one handsome?"

From Shawnee's previous description, he guessed that the "tall one" was this GW character who had come on to his wife. He pulled away from Ingrid then realized that Shawnee would soon be required to return to the scene of the spill. He could not expect her to come back to this, so he quickly scooped up the mess and returned to the kitchen. She was still holding on to the sink.

The clock was reporting the time to be only 8:30. He knew she could never stay for the rest of her shift-so resolutely he pulled the fire alarm.

As the building quickly emptied, the 2 male models were among the last to leave. The snow had continued more heavily since about 6 pm and it was making travel very difficult. The local volunteer fire fighters were on the scene within 20 minutes but found no fire. Officially, the alarm was attributed to a faulty wire. Tim, however, never told anyone that he had pulled the alarm. The snow and the 20 minute interval before the firemen arrived effectively iced the "art show" and without much thought, Ingrid declared the evening over.

Their night at the Lobo's Den having ended, he took her home.

She was really traumatized-she did not speak- just sat quietly looked at the fire in the fireplace, patted Grayboy and held Goodness and Mercy.

Finally, she said, "I just can't do that anymore. I will have to turn in my 2 weeks notice on Tuesday."

Tim just held her and stroked her hair, kissing her softly.

He knew that the Krauses would be gone next weekend and that if he could cover for Shawnee on Tuesday, maybe things would blow over. Still he was amazed what he had seen- she's really right-this stuff is not normal.

It snowed all night and Tim awoke that Sunday to the sound of his truck starting. He looked at the clock, it was 8:30- over the oven door she had written a note-

"Breakfast is in the oven, I didn't want to wake you, I <u>HAVE</u> to go to church- don't worry, I'll be careful with the truck- Be back around Noon-LOVE, Me

Chapter 19

The snow kept most Tye River congregants home that Sunday. Since the parsonage was next to the church, Pastor Don and Martha were there and perhaps six others.

Shawnee had no trouble getting to church- Tim's truck was sure footed if somewhat light in the tail end.

The small group of faithful sang some of the great old hymns of the faith, _A Mighty_ **Fortress Is Our God** , **Jesus is Tenderly Calling, Blessed Assurance,** _and_ **Just As I Am.** Pastor Don 's sermon was about being faithful and the small offering was barely enough to cover the electricity bill- _but_ more importantly, Shawnee was able to get prayer and counsel from the Trumbels. She also promised to come back on Wednesday, with or without Tim.

The snow continued all afternoon Sunday and all day Monday.

Tim and Shawnee did little talking about anything except the house and how to redo it. Nothing was said about the events at the Lobo's Den at all-which Tim found peculiar. Secretly Tim (and probably Shawnee) hoped that the snowstorm would effectively shutdown Route 29 and thus close the Den. That is precisely what happened.

13 inches of snow caused all local business on the earth's surface to shut down. Unfortunately for Tim, the same was not true for subterranean work. He was expected on time for work on both Monday and Tuesday.

As Wednesday approached, the weather continued to be bad. The temperature stayed well below freezing so the roads remained poor. As Tim came in the door just after 6, Shawnee and company swarmed over him with kisses, hugs, licks, and purring. Everyone but Tim had been virtually snow bound since late Saturday. Tim was weary from the 111/2 hours he had just put in,
"Timmy," she cooed, "do you know what tonight is?"
Quickly without a trace of panic, Tim responded, "Our anniversary?"
"Nice try, McGregor. That is 6 months from now. Want to try again?"
"Your birthday?"
"You're getting warmer- that's a month from now. Tell you what though, to take the pressure off of you – you can give me my birthday present tonight."
"But I haven't got you anything yet and the stores are probably all closed still due to the roads."
"What I want, they don't sell in stores."
"Why Shawnee McGregor, I never thought you'd talk that way- especially in front of the children!"
Blushing, she poked him in the ribs and said," Now you stop. I just want 2 hours of your time- at the Tye River church."
He was caught and he knew it. Had it been a week already? He hated being boxed in but really did not see the need to go out especially in these conditions.
"I doubt if anyone will show up- it's really too dangerous without a 4 wheel drive."
"Which we have. Come on, get changed- remember that we have this Friday off and I may just shut down that den of iniquity on Saturday since the Krauses will be gone."

"I just don't think that going out is a good idea- couldn't we try another time?"

Her face- now very downcast, said to him that he had failed her-again.

She took his keys, kissed him and headed off into the frigid air.

At Tye River, the number was even smaller than Sunday and there was no power. By candle light the faithful brought forth prayer concerns and remembered that even a small light can bring about great change. The small church was quite cold but the warmth of other believers brought her great comfort.

It was after 10 when she got home- Tim was sound asleep- there would be no discussion tonight of what separated them.

Sunrise on Thursday brought yet another round of snow. Since there wasn't much to do outside, Shawnee occupied herself with sketching the home that they soon hoped to be living in. While detailing in her mind, what each room would require to refurbish and update, she toyed with a ball of yarn, rolling it between the kittens.

Sitting by the fire, with Goodness and Mercy, she then calculated the number of boards and 2x4's she thought they would need so that when the stores did open, she could put price tags on her dreams.

Since Tim and Shawnee both had the day off Friday, she made his favorite meal Thursday night then dusted off her favorite video tape and they watched Shenandoah.

Afterward Tim complimented Jimmy Stewart for lending advice to the average man trying to figure out women in general and wives specifically.

"We are not so different. We just want attention and love."

"Well, you definitely have my attention and the night is still young."

The falling snow, the fire, the kittens, the dog, all this leant itself an ideal evening at home.

Early the next morning, they decided to go to Mae's house, so everyone piled into the truck, or tried to. Goodness and Mercy had no chance to make it, which was fine with Grayboy, the snow now measuring over 17 inches. Carefully bundling them up, Shawnee carried them to the truck. Once they got to Mae's there would be lots of room to run. No one seemed to remember that there would be no power at Mae's so Tim built a fire and much of their time was spent coming back to it.

Shawnee's memory proved to be accurate and they enjoyed visualizing what the house would eventually look like. Kicking the cabin fever bug was always challenging but this outing, short as it was, was worthwhile.

When they got home, Tim idly turned on the TV. There was live footage on all the network channels coming from Washington, D.C. of the annual celebration of the Roe v. Wade case, the case that had made abortion legal in the USA.

"Come here," Tim cried out- "quick!"

Setting the kittens' bowl down, she got to the TV in time to see the honored guests on the center stage. Next to several Hollywood stars and politicians were the Krauses, though they were not identified.

"I should have known! I should have known! This explains everything. Those people are evil- I knew it!"

"Now wait a minute- they are entitled to have their opinion, just because they support abortion, that doesn't make them evil."

She hated to admit it but it really had been coming for a long time. She promised herself to keep cool and be patient with Tim- he could not see things yet for what they were.

She started slowly, " Tim, is there life before birth?" she asked as she turned off the TV.

"What? I don't know...I ...uh... I guess so, why?"

"When our daughter died, why were you sad?"

"Why was I sad?" What kind of question is that?"

"Were you sad for me, us or her?"

"Why for us, for you and her- but what has that got..."

"Were you sad because she didn't live?"

"Of course, I mean absolutely!"

"So she was alive but died?"

The light finally went on in Tim's mind- of course their daughter had been alive- they had even buried her- he could see that he had never really thought through the issue of life before birth. "I'm sorry, I see what you are saying- yes, there is life before birth."

She breathed deeply and thought to herself- we are halfway home – well here, goes-help me Lord.

"Tim is there life *after* death?"

"I guess tonight we have to solve all of life's mysteries- yeah, I guess so."

"Is there a real heaven and a real hell?"

"Yeah, I suppose."

"Where is our daughter tonight- heaven or hell?"

"In heaven, I reckon, though God only knows."

"So there is a God?"

"Look, do we have to talk about this stuff now- can't we talk later?"

Ignoring his question, she began again.

"Our daughter who lived within me, never drew the first breath on her own, she died, where is she now?"

"With God I suppose- please can we talk about this some other time?"

She knew that the door was closing so she decided to back off. She nodded but added, "Tim, I want you to know that I know where I will be 1 second after I'm dead. Can you say the same? Please think about it, ok?"

They kissed and it was quiet for a while.

Facing another day at home tomorrow, but with Tim by her side, she decided that the best thing they could do on this Friday night was to bundle up and ...

"C'mon McGregor- let's go sledding!"

"Sledding!? You're on!" This was the spontaneous, fun girl he had married. Oh, how he had missed those simpler days.

2 hours and several big spills coming down courthouse hill later, they found themselves warming up in front of the fire and watching Grayboy fend off the kittens.

"Coming to bed?" he asked.

"In a while, I want to read my Bible- I haven't read it today."

Today-Tim thought-I guess I should do the same-naaaa... maybe later.

"That is excellent! We would be thrilled to meet with him as soon as possible," said the balding man.

"Well?"

"15 minutes- Capital Square Apartments- Number 106."

The well-appointed apartment of the Lithuanian translator was the perfect spot for the three men to pour over Mae's diary.

The translator got right to the point- "I was very disturbed by what this woman wrote, is she willing to verify everything?"

"Sadly, she has recently deceased. What, may I ask, was most disturbing?" prodded the handsome, well-dressed man.

"This is barbarity at its absolute lowest point... Here rather than have me read it to you, I have had copies made so that you may read it for yourselves."

For the next 20 minutes, there were few sounds emanating from Apartment 106 accept pages turning. Gradually groans and heads shaking were added.

"If we can build from this document we can finally close the loop."

"It is hard to imagine what that little lady endured- we owe it to her to seek justice."

The 2 paid the translator and left Apartment 106. They had now some testimony, despite the fact that the witness was dead. Would they be able to piece together enough to continue?

Back in Lovingston, Shawnee McGregor- made a decision- she knew that the snow was but a brief respite from having to return to the *Devil's Den*- as she was now calling it- either she quit with Tim's permission or secretly she might file a suit against the Krauses- but who would know how to go about doing that stuff? Maybe the Trumbels could help- and by the way, another Sunday was coming – would this be the Sunday that Tim finally took her back to Tye River?

Saturday was a virtual repeat of Friday and they almost exactly retraced their steps except they had to do laundry and shop.

Tim was not sure if it was just the effects of being shut in for several days or not, but it seemed that men of all ages were starring at his wife. He caught himself admiring her form and her ways – she was so easy to look at and such a sweet girl- no wonder everyone starred. He so wanted to please her but his pride seemed to be always getting in his way.

Chapter 20

This became the winter and spring of her discontent. She absolutely abhorred working at the Lobo's Den, using each and every excuse she could think of to stay away from Ingrid.

The McGregors had briefly discussed their predicament- they needed Dr. Jo in getting legal help so that Mae's house could be theirs', thus Shawnee had to continue working so as to not anger the Krauses. With no written documentation at all that Maria Ludlov was in any way connected to Shawnee Trace Overton McGregor, they needed to stay on the Krauses' good side.

Shawnee prayed a lot more and spent each Wednesday night with the Trumbels, who upheld her in prayer, helping her cope with Ingrid.

Despite her best efforts, Tim would not go to church with her. They split their Sundays either at some overnight motel-the routine was leave after she got off at 10 pm, drive to some fairly local motel and then spend Sunday racing around some theme park, historic battlefield or beach site, then hurry home so that he could report for work at 5:30 the following Monday morning. They did have day trips on the 7th and 16th of March (company holidays) - but there wasn't much time alone together. On Sundays when they were home, she went to Tye River alone, while he slept in or worked on his project car. She felt that Tim would eventually come to the Lord but each time she tried to bring up the subject, Tim could not be more evasive. There also didn't seem to be any communication forthcoming from Dr. Jo, but at least once a month, Tim asked to see the Doctor- but to no avail.

So as February became March and March became April, despite her best hopes, things stayed pretty much unchanged. He *had* remembered her birthday by presenting her with the 70 % completed 1932 Chevy, but her true desire, getting him to meet and accept Jesus, remained unanswered.

Tim for his part felt that he was being stiff-armed by Dr. Jo, while growing farther and farther from his wife. He began to think of ways to draw her closer to him.

Wednesday, March 18th, Tim got home late and she had already gone to church. Her note-

Timmy-I missed you today-I have gone to Tye River- come on if you feel up to it- dinner is in the oven-should be home by 8:30-9-Love, Me

He switched on the TV in time to see Mother Theresa. She was addressing a room full of journalists and politicians. 'I thought she was dead'- Tim mused.

Mother Theresa was saying, "Abortion is the greatest destroyer of peace today."

She was greeted with a standing ovation. The camera panned the entire room. Everyone was standing and applauding the gracious lady. Everyone except the 6 people sharing the platform with her. Tim immediately recognized Bill and Hillary Clinton, Al and Tipper Gore and Dr. Jo and Ingrid Krause. All were still seated and all were frowning.

Mother Theresa continued: "And if we accept that a mother can kill even her own child, how can we tell other people not to kill one another?" More applause.

"Please don't kill the child. I want the child. Please give me the child. I am willing to accept any child who would be aborted and to give that child to a married couple who will love the child and be loved by the child."

Another standing ovation, except for the scowling three couples who sat stone faced on the dais.

The announcer came on and reminded viewers that the footage was from the 1994 National Prayer Breakfast and that Mother Theresa had indeed passed away. At about that time, the '700 Club' logo scrolled across the screen. " I might have known," he thought. "She was watching the 700 Club before she went to church."

When she came home that evening, they had their usual Wednesday evening discussion about church.

"You know I don't mind you going to church on Sunday morning but this Wednesday night stuff- is this really necessary? I mean what is wrong with spending Wednesday night here with me? We do pretty well, why do you have to go?"

"Tim, we have this discussion all the time, it's not about church, Pastor Don or Martha, it's about Jesus- I asked Him to save me and he has."

"Save you from what? ERWACHE, the Lobo's Den, me? We do all right; there are plenty of people who would love to have our income, our job security and our healthcare plan, our early retirement plan, the regular pay raises. We love each other, don't we? Then why do we need God, or church or any of it?"

"Tim, did you get any of that that you just mentioned on your own? God had a plan through all of this .You would understand better and more if you would go with me..." Silence surrounded them as they went to bed.

With discouragement facing him every morning, and his dear wife hating her job, he decided on March 19th, to take a walk during his lunch hour. He had never heard back from Rolf about the VW in shaft 16, so he made his way deep down to the point where his auger had broken through.

Sure enough, the auger had never been retrieved and just beyond its point was the old bug, still in 2 feet of water. He took some time and studied the car's overall condition. Despite the water, the car looked new. He was puzzled because there was no structural damage, it just might run, except...except there was another car just behind it ...Tim judged it to be a Ford

Maverick, it also appeared to be in great shape. Both cars had evidently been there for a long time. In the glow of his helmet lamp he could make out the form of still a third car, this one appeared to a foreign sports car maybe a Fiat Spyder. Again, the car appeared to be in very good condition. As he walked toward the rear of this, the third car in line, he couldn't tell about its rear because a 4th car was behind it. The lunch hour rapidly passing, he decided to return to work and ask about the VW later.

Elsewhere in Lovingston that same evening:
"You are certain of this?"
"Quite, he was in that tunnel for 8 1/2 minutes."
"This issue was to have been resolved months ago- our security is at stake!"
"Security has not been breached and...."
"That is enough out of your incompetent mouth about security – how dare you not to have dealt with this?"
Rolf had no answer.
"I will be forced to handle this due to your malfeasance. Get out of my sight!"

Dawn of March 20th found Tim underground and Shawnee laying in bed thinking about where their marriage had taken them in just over ½ year. They were planning a big move. The issue of children had not re-entered conversation since the baby was lost. Church attendance was something he would not consider, while to her it was required for sanity's sake. He had been promoted and each was being paid well. She hated her job but as it turned out, over the course of the winter, Ingrid was traveling more and seldom at the Lobo's Den more than once or twice a week. Shawnee had developed a close friendship with Martha Trumbel, Pastor Don's wife. They enjoyed each other's company both at church and on their frequent trips both shopping and sightseeing.

Martha was the more mature of the 2 spiritually, constantly encouraging Shawnee through the hard times as well as the good. Whenever the 2 went shopping, they were painfully aware that they were being stared at. Both young women were in their early 20's and while Shawnee was stunning, not a few leered at tall and athletic Martha.

This being Friday, Shawnee dozed off, but awoke 1½ hours later, dreading her shift at the Lobo's Den, when the phone rang.

"Hi, Shawnee? its me-Don's busy this morning, you wanna go to North Garden with me?"

"Sure-what's the mission this time?"

"Funny you should say mission- Don and I are sponsoring some mission kids in Thailand and we thought that they might like some fudge-you know I'm not much of a cook- so we thought about buying some fudge from the Corner Store at North Garden and shipping it to our MKs."

"You know Martha, we could make some here if you want to try-but then on second thought, I'd like to get out of the house –so why not-let's go. Are you picking me up or do you want me to come get you?"

"I'll come get you- can you be ready in say- ½ hour?"

"Sure thing- just as long as I'm back by 3:30 so I can get ready to be abused... I mean... to go to work. Wanna stop by Mae's house either coming or going?"

"Now that sounds like a plan –see you in a few."

Shawnee reflected on their friendship. Martha was like the older sister that she had never had. They both liked many of the same things and after meeting Goodness and Mercy, Martha had convinced Pastor Don that they too needed a pet. So far, a fish was all that they had agreed on but she felt sure that as the weather improved, prolonged exposure to Grayboy and the "yellow peril" would get Pastor Don to see things her way.

Sometimes they just sat and had girl talk sessions- Martha was so vital to Shawnee's mental health- so few people have such close friends- Shawnee just treasured their times together .

Their ride up to North Garden was uneventful, but while they were there a scene inside the store struck them. A man and his wife worked diligently behind the counter making sandwiches and milkshakes to order. Between them, in a special wheelchair sat their invalid daughter. Neither woman knew the circumstances of these parents but it was obvious that they deeply loved their child.

"Martha, those people really love their daughter."

"That's the agape love that Jesus has for all of us. He loves us unconditionally .I imagine that if you were to look up the word parents in the dictionary, you would see a picture of those two people. They truly love their little girl."

Things grew silent as Shawnee thought of how Ingrid would have viewed the girl. *'Useless eater, no reason to live, no quality of life, why should she live'.*

"Hey, you ok, too much fudge?"

"No, I'm fine- just thinking too much for my own good- say could we stop at the Covesville Antique Store?"

"Time to put the dreams into motion-maybe find some antiques for your new house?"

"Do you mind?"

"Not at all."

They were upstairs on the porch looking at a pie safe when the lady owner   downstairs called up to them-

"Is one of you Shawnee McGregor?"

"I am."

" You have a phone call down stairs."

They hurried downstairs- wondering who could be calling.

It was someone from ERWACHE.

"Yes? How? Where is he? Can I talk to him?"

The color had completely drained from her face. Martha held her by the elbow as she concluded, "I'll be right there."

"There's been an accident. Tim is badly hurt. They have him at the infirmary."

Martha thanked the proprietor and they headed for the Trumbel's mini-van. Suddenly fudge did not seem very important.

On the way to Lovingston- Martha called Don on her cell phone and he was waiting for them outside the Lobo's Den, when they arrived in Lovingston.

Shawnee led the Trumbels through the kitchen toward the sideways tram.

Chapter 21

Tim had just emerged from the mine and his eyes were adjusting to the sunlight when suddenly he was hit hard in the face. There was great pain and he fell hitting his head hard on the tram rail. He had lain there unconscious for some time before a mute worker discovered him.

When Shawnee and the Trumbels entered the infirmary, they were required to don sterile over garments before they could see Tim. What struck the Trumbels was that there was no one there to explain what had happened.

They entered the Intensive Care Unit there were 3 doctors somewhat passively studying Tim from 8-10 feet away.

Shawnee hastily said- "What's going on? What happened?"

The 3 doctors impassively turned and shushed the new comer.

"We require silence- there was an accident. He will recover almost fully."

"Almost? What do you mean?" Shawnee virtually screamed.

Again, the physicians shushed her.

" The saker attack was inadvertent. This man will recover all but his left eye."

Shawnee began to weep. Martha comforted her friend.

"Don, what is a saker?"

"I think it's a Eur-Asian falcon, it's used for hunting." He turned toward the physicians and asked if Tim was sedated or just unconscious.

"We are not sure, and just what is your function here?" they asked of Pastor Trumbel.

"We are friends of the McGregors and this is his wife."

"If you must visit-be brief," said the one woman doctor as they left the room.

"Not sure if Tim is sedated? What kind of a doctor doesn't know if his patient is sedated or not?" Martha asked.

The 3 friends clustered around Tim.

"Timmy? Can you hear me? I'm here and so are Pastor Don and Martha. Can you hear me?"

There was no change in his condition for several minutes then suddenly his hands moved as if trying to fend off something. Tim opened his eye and gazed warily around. Shawnee kissed him and held his hand. The Trumbels pulled back allowing them to have some time together. They left the room and inquired of the nurse on duty what could be expected for Tim's near future.

"Except the left eye, he will recover."

"When can he be released?"

"I do not have that information."

"Can his wife stay here with him?"

"I do not have that information."

"Who is the doctor in charge here?"

"I do not have that information."

"Does he need blood or is there anything that we can do to help?"

"I do not have that information."

Puzzled they nodded and returned to Tim's room.

Martha approached Shawnee and noticed that Tim was no longer conscious.

The Trumbels and Shawnee prayed for Tim and for guidance. Since there did not seem to be any comprehensible answer forth, coming- they decided that Pastor Don should stay with Tim while Martha took Shawnee back to the parsonage.

Elsewhere at the ERWACHE infirmary, a phone was used to convey:
"Quite sure."
"Recovery time?"
"About 4-5 weeks- however the fall has led to a system disconnect- this needs to be reestablished toward the end of the recuperation. We feel that he will not be a threat."
"Understood- write a 5 week released from work pass and send him home."
"Very well, sir."

Tim appeared in and out of consciousness throughout the night. Since there was no provision for visitors, Pastor Trumbel sat on the floor and nodded off and on. Twice a nurse came in to check his vital signs and change his IVs, but no doctor came in through that dreadful first night. Tim was not fully conscious until the following morning and then wasn't very sure of what happened.

From what could be pieced together, apparently as Tim emerged from the mine, one of Dr. Jo's hunting falcons had attacked him. He had no real memory of the event, nor did he remember anything at the infirmary.

Shawnee wept throughout the night but with dawn, she could not wait to see Tim. Martha had called in for her on Friday and made sure that the animals were fed on the way back to the infirmary on Saturday morning.

Shawnee and Martha had to walk from the Lobo's Den since the tram was not running on Saturday.

As they entered the room where Tim had spent a painful night, they were again bothered by the absence of a doctor.

The nurse, who seemed to be routinely caring for a man who had just tragically lost his left eye, barely noticed the trio entering.

"Excuse us, but is there a doctor that can explain what to expect?"

"No." She blandly handed the stunned wife a slip of paper stating that Tim was excused from work for up to 5 weeks, and left the room.

"This is unbelievable. I have never seen anything like this," Pastor Trumbel whispered to the women. "Please let's not get Tim agitated- since he is apparently free to go- let's get him home- or at least out of here."

They eased Tim into a sitting position and while Martha attempted to get more information from the front desk nurse, Don and Shawnee dressed Tim.

Tim was very groggy but knew his wife and hugged her repeatedly. She tried to be strong for him but without the massive former linebacker's aid, she wasn't sure if she could have handled her stricken husband.

Martha got no more information from the desk nurse and collectively the trio carried Tim all the way back to the Lobo's Den - then out the front door. As they passed through the Den, Martha left a note stating that Shawnee would not be in that night.

Saturday afternoon became Saturday evening, the Trumbels provided food and care for the ailing McGregors.

As night fell, Shawnee insisted that her friends return to their home, stating that she and Tim would be all right.

Before leaving, they prayed for Tim, that he would have the strength that only God could provide in this terrible trial.

Shawnee kissed both of her friends and returned to care for her husband.

The phone rang. "Hello. This is she. I really can't talk- perhaps in a week or more- we have had a tragedy here- thank you."

She turned toward Tim and before she could do anything, the phone rang again.

"Hello. That's right. How did...?"

"In this small town, news travels fast- I'm sure adequate care was provided- we will be thinking about you. Come see us."

"Fat chance"- thought Shawnee-how dare that man...?

"Who was that?" called Tim weakly.

With those first spoken words, she ran to his side and held him. Together they cried.

Later that evening, she related what she knew of the events of the past 24 hours. "That first call was some foreign man with a survey or something. The second call was from the right reverend Inke, pretending to care about us again."

Tim's spirits plummeted. "How could this happen? We were going along so well, how can you love a handicapped man, a freak....?" He was crying.

"Now you listen to me Mr. McGregor. I married you for better or for worse, in sickness and in health, 'til death do us part. None of that has changed. You are my husband and I love you. We are not giving up. Do you understand me?"

"Yes ma'am. I love you too." They hugged each other then began to cry again. The weeping was interrupted by Grayboy trying to get to his master. As he got between the couple, Goodness and Mercy climbed the bed covers and ran to Shawnee's side. Despite the tragedy of their circumstances, they began to laugh and the closest thing to an interspecies group hug carried them into Sunday morning.

With dawn, Shawnee got up, fed the animals and began to fix breakfast.

"Trace, what are you doing- why aren't you getting ready for church?"

"How can I think about anything but you?" she cried.

"Come on, *we* are going to be late."

"We? You said we!"

"I know I did- come on help me dress and you'll have to drive but I've been needing to go with you for a long time."

She hugged and kissed him, then slowly helped him get ready. Despite his enthusiasm, he was very apprehensive and very unsteady. What would people think? Would he scare children? Would Shawnee be embarrassed to be with him? Would he be able to work again? Would he be expected to work again? What would normal life be without seeing things on his left? He had no answers as they climbed into the truck.

She drove them slowly toward Tye River church. The trip was a blur to him. He was glad to be out of the house but he grew very dizzy by the time they got parked and out of the truck.

"I don't want you to miss the service but I need to sit down, somewhere that's quiet." The small church library was just off the sanctuary and there was a comfortable chair there.

"We can stay here- there's even a speaker in here so we can hear the..."

"Not we, I want you to go on to the service- I'll be in after I rest for awhile. Now go on, I'll be ok." He kissed her and reluctantly she left.

The service did not go well. Unfortunately, Pastor Don had been so tied up helping the McGregors that he had not practiced his sermon adequately. Martha's music was also off just enough to be noticeable. Pastor Trumbel's message concerned Caleb and Joshua – their strength during a time when everyone else said there was no hope.

To make matters worse- some of the recently disenfranchised *"established families"*, were in attendance and had requested a church business meeting at the conclusion of the service.

Shawnee sat with Kristin and her sister- often apprehensively gazing over her shoulder, hoping that Tim would soon join her.

Kristin had checked on him after the offering and he was sitting peacefully. The invitation hymn, *Only Trust Him*, was concluding and still no Tim.

Now the business meeting was commencing, briefly Shawnee forgot about Tim because of the onslaught facing the Trumbels.

"Now, take today's sermon, please," said one of the Russells to howling approval from the *old families*. "Really, how much preparation did you do?"

"That sermon was as flat as dishwater," huffed the oldest Davenport. "And don't get me started on the quality of the music."

Not embarrassed but definitely riled, Martha Trumbel started, "And just what was wrong with..." she stopped as Pastor Don cut her off by grabbing her arm.

The elder Russell said, "I propose that we vote on this couple again."

"Now just a minute" piped up Shawnee.

"Ahhhh, the voice of the barmaid..." chimed in some irritating Davenport man. "Honey, why don't you go sleep it off?"

Shawnee began to speak but was frozen by what she saw-everyone turned in unison to see a one eyed man moving unsteadily down the aisle.

"You all don't know me but one more word about my wife and one of you is going to meet my fists in person," he said glaring at the Davenport irritant.

"I'm Tim McGregor. I lost my eye on Friday. No one in this church can say a thing against this Pastor or his wife. He stayed with me all night Friday and his wife cared for my wife that same night. All day Saturday, they helped us through our loss. The Trumbels fed us, they cared for our pets, they us showed the most love I have ever received-this from 2 people that I really do not know. But I think I know their hearts- this couple shows their love by action- you would be greatly mistaken thinking that Don Trumbel was ill-prepared- they sacrificed for me and my wife. I am not a member here, but I know the Trumbels- they are good people. I am not sure what a Christian is supposed to act like because outside my own wife, I do not know many Christians, but the Pastor and his wife are real people, they cared for even me, a stranger. Please don't turn them out." With that, he stumbled and collapsed into one of the pastor's chairs.

"That was very touching," said the sassy leader of the Davenports, "but we don't need these kinds of people in our church. A barmaid and a disabled man. The real issue is what do we believe in. The preacher and his wife take the Bible to be true word for word. Any logical modern person knows that is foolish. Take the story about Jonah- who could possibly believe that ? "

Shawnee who had been tending to her husband, was about to speak when the veteran from Omaha Beach arose and moved forward.

"You may think I'm old fashioned-but the scripture teaches the Golden Rule. If the Trumbels are being criticized for caring for others, then I would like someone to explain why Jesus came to earth. Was it to please man? And we had better be careful when we pretend that the Bible isn't true. To do that, you are doing it at your own peril. This couple obviously loves God and His Son. They are good people and there is no reason that they should leave. As to who is the right kind of person for our church, let me put it this way- if they go, I go. Oh and by the way, Jesus himself told the story of Jonah so if Jesus' word is not true then why are any of us here?"

With that, the old soldier received a standing ovation- except from the *"established families"* who stormed out. Shawnee diverted her attention from attending to Tim long enough to whistle her approval.

Chapter 22

Having bested the most recent Tye River crisis, the McGregors settled in to life at a slower pace. Tim was not expected to work and he told Shawnee she should not have to either. Still it came as quite a surprise on the following Tuesday as Shawnee was shopping at CVS, to have her name called over the store PA system.

Since it was early in the morning, Megan was not yet there and Thelma perhaps did not remember Shawnee from the events last fall.

Fearing the worst, remembering the last phone call when she and Tim had been separated, she answered the store's phone with great reservation.

"Hello?"

Momentarily relieved to hear a woman's voice, her blood boiled quickly thereafter. It was Ingrid, calling from Thailand.

"Yes. I need you to open the Den for the next 2 weeks while I am avay."

"I just can't do that" she protested.

"Certainly you can and you must."-cited Ingrid matter-of- factly. "There is no one else. It is very necessary for you to as you are told."

"Well, I know to you that it may be *very necessary*- but my husband just lost his eye working for *your* company. If you have to fire me-do so now, but it is more important to me to help him recuperate than to open that place. I believe that the corporation is not going to be financially ruined by me not opening the store."

"I see. Very well then, I shall make a note of this conversation and report it to Dr.Jo. You may want to reconsider."

"And I may not," protested Shawnee.

"So noted." Click. The phone went dead.

Shawnee looked around to see if anyone was listening. No one was within earshot except a balding man who seemed engrossed in his newspaper at the lunch counter.

As she drove home she keep mulling over in her mind- how did she find me at the CVS? All the way from Thailand? Is Lovingston really that small that she could call around until she found me?

She opened the door to their home to find Tim and the animals sleeping. The answering machine showed no incoming calls in her absence. I wonder, she started...

Her thoughts were interrupted by the phone ringing. She quickly picked it up, hoping that Tim could continue to rest.

Quietly, she said, "This is she. It really isn't convenient for me to talk now. Please give me a call back in 2 weeks. By the way, what does this concern- we have paid our bills and I don't know of any thing we need to ... Oh, I see. My aunt's home? Well, fine, call me back in a week. Thank you."

March became April and with each day, Tim grew a little more steady and accustomed to his handicap. He drove over a couple of times to the restoration shop, chatting with some of the mechanics there- basically trying to get back to a normal pace.

The Lobo's Den remained closed and Shawnee had no intention of reopening it until Tim was steady enough on his own.

The Krauses did send a get well card from Jamaica but Tim was perplexed by its content-hoping his broken leg would heal!

"I told you Timmy! They could not care less about you or us!"

He was beginning to see things her way.

As the days went by, he was deeply depressed. Tim had a very difficult time with depth perception and he considered requesting a transfer to an above ground station when the time came to return to work.

Each Wednesday night Shawnee went to Tye River for Bible study and Tuesday and Thursday she spent with Martha. The 2 young women often ministered to the poor or just visited shut ins- sometimes allowing themselves an ice cream cone from the North Garden store or from Colleen. Their time together was therapeutic for Shawnee, yet she couldn't help but think about how Tim needed fellowship and nurturing as well.

On Sundays, they both attended Tye River and Pastor Don intonated secretly to Shawnee that he saw small changes in Tim. From that conversation sprang an idea- he would spend Tuesday mornings with Tim, provided Shawnee thought it a good idea.

So on the second Tuesday of April, the Trumbels climbed out of their mini-van and took each of the McGregors in different directions. While the women went shopping in the Trumbel's minivan, the men drove over to the state fish hatchery at Montebello. Tim was still adjusting to his condition, depth perception being a major concern, so he let Pastor Don drive the Chevy pickup.

They climbed up and in, not a small feat with the 10-inch lift that Tim had engineered.

The truck roared to life and the driver lit the tires with the first touch of the accelerator.

"Wow! "Exclaimed the preacher. "How much horsepower is your engine pushing?"

"I had it dynoed last summer. On pump gas, without the turbo charger, about 850. With the turbo and little taste of nitrous about 1400. I've never gotten a ticket but it would be real easy to."

"This thing is awesome."

"Probably the fastest in the valley for its size. It won several trophies- I have about 18,000 in the engine and another 4 in the transmission."

Pastor Trumbel reflected to himself about earthly treasures and bigger barns.

The day was unusually warm even for April.

On the way, Don Trumbel spoke not in preacher's terms but of sports teams, fishing and their wives. This was a side that few people saw. He knew that Tim was a fisherman so he felt like the state hatchery would be something of interest. His guess proved correct- Tim got excited about springtime and fishing- precisely what Don had hoped- something to keep his mind off of his troubles.

"Tim, I'm not a fisherman but I am a fisher of men."

"Pastor, you'd better explain that one," exclaimed Tim, admiring the beautiful rainbow trout in tank number 6.

"You may know that Jesus hung out with fishermen. He taught them to fish for men- to get people interested in things beyond this life. As we look all around us, at these beautiful fish and the wonderful spring flowers, all this is nice but just a sample of what life will be like in heaven."

Tim's defensive shield was on its way up.

"You two have had a really rough fall and winter- I can't think of anyone who has suffered in more ways than you 2. And yet, God still loves you and wants you to draw near to him-Shawnee already has. How about you?"

"I can't... I just don't think I am worthy... I mean, I 'm not good enough... I can't see how Jesus could love me... I'm just a common good ol' boy... How could I earn a place in heaven? ...I'm just not a good person."

They were strolling up a trail admiring the beauty of the weather but a convenient log brought them to a halt. The forest service attendants waved as they drove by the men. The hatchery had just closed. They sat and continued their discussion.

"What if I told you that no one is worthy of heaven." Don started.

"I'd say- you don't know my wife. For that matter, I think both you and your wife are worthy."

"Tim, at the risk of offending you, no one is worthy including the 3 people you just named. I don't want to bowl you over with scripture so let's just start with this: "If you died tonight, where would your soul be tomorrow morning?"

"I guess it would be with God."

"Your wife, my wife and I all know for sure we would be with God. Would you like to join us?"

Tim gulped hard- this sounded like decision time.

"Let me put it another way. God's word tells us that we will be able to see each other after we die. But, can you imagine not being able to touch Shawnee again- seeing her only from a distance and being eternally separated from her."

The only sound was the rushing water in the nearby stream. Tim reflected on Don's words. Not be able to hold Shawnee again? See her but not touch her. A tear welled up in his good eye.

He didn't know what to say but he didn't have to say anything. The pastor continued.

"I'm going to walk you down what is called the Roman road, ok?"

Tim nodded.

"The scripture in the book-*OUCH!!!!* Exclaimed the young preacher. "What in the????...."

They both arose and peered at Don's right calf. Affixed to it was large copperhead-it's fangs were snagged in the preacher's jeans.

Tim grabbed it by it's tail and pulled the creature free. He frantically looked for a rock or stick to kill the animal but to no avail. It slithered off as silently as it had approached.

Pastor Don was holding his leg. Tim took his belt off and fastened it snuggly above the wound.. Tim pulled out his pocketknife cutting jean fabric then bent to examine the bite.

"Pastor, this is serious. Forgive me if this hurts." He cut 2 x's just above the fang marks and then attempted to suck out the poison.

The angle of the bite made it very difficult for Tim to help.

After a few minutes, it was obvious that only a small amount of venom was being recovered.

Tim helped the former linebacker toward the truck He tried to remember all the procedures for treating a snakebite. He laid the preacher in the middle of the seat head up but leg down, the belt still fastened around his calf.

Quickly starting the truck, Tim immediately floored it. He tried to comfort Don by talking about sports, fishing and Martha. But as he sped toward Route 29, Tim became increasingly agitated. He felt dizzy from the curves that he had been taking at 80 miles per hour. Despite trying to keep Don in conversation, it sounded to Tim that Don might be entering shock. Tim dare not peer toward Don- he was having a hard enough time driving with his one eye.

Suddenly they rounded a curve and narrowly missed a hay wagon stopped and blocking most of the road.

Tim hit the horn but then realized that the wagon was stopped because a herd of cattle was leisurely crossing the road, going from one pasture to another.

Turning to look at Don, it seemed to Tim that he was sleeping, but the heavy sweating and his general appearance was ashen.

Tim dropped the truck into 4-wheel drive, blew the horn and forced his way past the wagon, narrowly missing several cows. The farmer was none other than the WWII veteran from D-Day. Frantically Tim rolled the window down low enough to shout "Snake Bite", floored the gas, the truck dug all 4 wheels into the soft shoulder then sped on.

Speed was of the essence now- Don needed medical attention immediately. Finally swerving onto Route 29, Tim realized that the closest hospital was in Charlottesville- perhaps 45 minutes away if he flew. He increased the speed of his pickup truck but realized that even with it, Don was in real danger.

Suddenly it hit Tim- the ERWACHE infirmary! That was the closest medical facility. He flew up Route 29 and his excessive speed drew the attention of the southbound Deputy Sheriff Terry Sullivan. The policeman spun his cruiser at the first opportunity but even the flashing light did not stop Tim. He turned into the Lovingston exit ramp and took it on 2 wheels. He slammed on brakes and ran toward the Lobo's Den. Just after he got in the door, Sheriff Sullivan, gun drawn, leapt from his car.

Ingrid Krause sat at the Espresso bar, reading a newspaper.

"Help me please! My friend has been bitten by a snake and needs medical care- is there anyone who can help me get him to the infirmary?" he said breathlessly.

"Timmy, what a pleasant surprise! You are looking just as good as new! Come here, sit beside me, and tell me what's wrong. It's not your wife is it?"

It was obvious to Tim that Ingrid had been drinking a lot more than Espresso. Her lack of response made him that much more fervent. "Please- a friend has been bitten by a poisonous snake- he needs help NOW!"

Now more alert, she said, "And just who is this person- an employee here?"

"He's the preacher at the Tye River church-please can you help him?"

"Absolutely not. The insurance regulations will not allow it, and we do not even know this person. It may be that he is one of those church people who handle snakes in their services. Besides, the snake probably wasn't even poisonous. Perhaps you could…"

Her words were drowned out by the sound of a helicopter over head.

Tim ran to the front porch in time to see a medivac copter land.

Four medics quickly loaded Don into the chopper and it flew off.

Tim was stunned by the speed with which the whole rescue occurred.

He approached Deputy Sheriff Sullivan and asked, "How could you act so quickly?"

"We are all aware of who has the fastest truck in the valley. I last clocked you at 145. I knew something was wrong. Plus some farmer on a cell phone complained about some wild driving by

a man wearing an eye patch. He also said he thought he heard something about a snake bite."
Tim blushed.
"So I played a hunch and called for a medivac- fortunately it looks like my hunch was correct."
At that instant, Ingrid called from the front porch- "If there is nothing that we can do to help, you will need to move those cars, it is bad for business."

Chapter 23

Due to Tim's excessive speed, and the great police work of Deputy Sullivan, Pastor Trumbel was completely recovered within 10 days. He had to miss a Sunday at Tye River preaching but was well enough to attend and thank the old veteran and Tim for their efforts.

During the days of recuperation, Tim and Shawnee drew closer to the Trumbels and actually got to repay them for some of the care given during Tim's recovery.

Tim was examined once a week at the infirmary and was told he was progressing as well as could be expected. There was something missing in these check-ups, compassion. Always the attending physician was very detached, never personable, almost as if attending to Tim was keeping them from something really important. No real information could be gleaned regardless of what anyone tried.

Usually after each visit, Shawnee was in tears. She knew how hard Tim had worked to function with just one eye. He was often depressed. He had been badly shaken up by what happened to Pastor Don. On their last checkup, Martha who had to be pre-approved by Ingrid accompanied them. As usual, no one at the infirmary knew anything but rudimentary information and no one seemed to be specializing in Tim's case.

Shawnee's usual response-tears- did not prevent her this time from making a bizarre discovery. As she and Martha accompanied Tim toward the tramline, she spotted through her tears a familiar face-at least a face that seemed familiar-Carly Addison.

She called out, " Carly. Carly Addison!?"

The bedraggled looking blonde that Shawnee addressed did not respond but instead climbed into a private tramcar with Rolf and then sped off.

"That was her. I know that was her. Did you see her Tim?"

"I couldn't see anything. My angle was wrong. Besides, I'm not sure I could identify her if she came up and bit me."

"What was the connection with that girl? I saw her"- Martha said.

"She supposedly fainted or something at the Lobo's Den- after coming on to my husband, I might add. Then she is supposed to have left town."

"Maybe it was a person who looked like her." Tim suggested.

"Maybe – but I still think she saw me and it was her-though she looked really bad."

The trio shrugged it off and made their way toward the sideways escalator. As they made their way through the Den, Ingrid called Shawnee aside.

"Despite the fact that tomorrow is a company holiday; you are expected to be available for a special assignment."

"Special assignment? What assignment?"

"We are having a large gathering at our home. You are needed to help with the guests. Several very important people will be there. I will send a car to get you. Your dress is on the hall coat rack-you may get it as you leave. That is all, you may leave."

"Ingrid- that is *not* all. My husband and I have had a hard time-we would like more time together and then there is the question about our house.."

"House? Oh, yes, now I remember - something about that weathered house that belonged to some relative-do you truly want that house?"

"I would like that more than most anything" she said.

"Very well, be ready at 4:30 tomorrow evening- you will be told about the house before the night is over."

Shawnee headed toward Martha and Tim, stopping to retrieve the dress that Ingrid had "arranged" for her to have.

"Guess what team. I have been selected to attend a big party tomorrow night at the Krause Castle. I'm told that if I'm a good girl and do what I'm told, we will have an answer to our house question before I become a pumpkin at midnight tomorrow," she said sarcastically.

She filled in the other 2 on the schedule as they walked home. Pastor Trumbel joined them and they all piled into the minivan for a trip to Lovingston's Golden Arches.

Elsewhere: In a small office in Alexandria,Virginia-

"We are at an impasse."

"So far, we have determined the veracity of the story but there are no living relatives, save the girl, and the wrong judge would throw out that connection. She must be told as soon as is possible."

"Have we any corroborating evidence tying together all the pieces?"

"The girl and her husband- we must develop them as assistants or otherwise we have no case."

"Time to drop deep cover?"

"Yes."

At 4:15 PM on Saturday, April 20th, there was a fashion show at the MacGregor house.

Grayboy, Tim, Goodness and Mercy all sat in rapt attention as Shawnee stepped into the small living room.

"Wow!" Tim whopped. "I can't let you go- you look *too good*! The canine and feline responses were equally enthusiastic.

"I'm serious —you have never looked so pretty-hey where's the back to that dress?"

She was in full blush now. "I don't like this, Timmy. It's like blackmail or something-I become eye candy again and then we can finally find out about Mae's. The whole thing is loony."

She applied the finishing touches; kissed, patted and hugged everyone and was picked up by long black limo.

Shawnee was not prepared for what she encountered at Castle Krause. All afternoon helicopters had been landing at the zeppelin port .One of the grand ships was tethered to the launch zone and most arrivals studied the monster first before traveling on to the castle. There were numerous Hollywood celebrities, 8 or more US Senators and ex-President and Mrs. Clinton, among the hundreds of guests.

The castle had perhaps 14 rooms on the first floor and even more upstairs. Shawnee was to serve the guests, answer questions and give directions. She soon picked up a common theme. This gathering was raising money for various liberal causes. In each room, there were hot conversations-political in nature- that she fled just as quickly as she could.

In one room, there was a large group of men, being addressed by Dr. Jo. He was lecturing about ERWACHE and it is plans for the future. Behind him on the wall hung a large sign- <u>PHOENIX-IT'S A NEW DAWN</u>.

She was very uneasy at each stop. The NARAL room (National Abortion Rights Action League) was being addressed by Ingrid.

"You will recall in days past the Renaissance Weekends that we had in South Carolina- today's event is a smaller, but no less important step toward a return to those days- before the reactionary Bush *took* power." The mention of President Bush's name brought forth boos and hisses. She spoke for a few more minutes and then turned to leave the dais, but not before kissing a young blonde woman on the mouth for several seconds.

Her sensibilities shattered, Shawnee stumbled into another room.

In this room, a meeting about the International Foundation for the Rights of the Child was being led by Hillary Clinton-sponsored by the Children's Defense Fund. "Remember it takes a village to raise a child"- she was saying. 'Chants of Pro

Woman, Pro Choice' were drowned out 'Run Hillary Run' filled the room

Shawnee was thinking, "Village my foot, that's not what *my* Bible says".

Hoping for a reprieve from all this bile, she rode the service elevator to the second floor kitchen. In the long upstairs hallway, there were several couples strolling and looking at the art that the Krauses had amassed. Only at the last moment, did she realize that all the couples were homosexual.

Still reeling and getting sicker by the minute, she entered a room that, like the ERWACHE room had only men. The men were clustered in small groups standing, admiring photographs that men in each group had. She noticed a young waiter, one of the boys from Woodrow Wilson- a mute, being poked and prodded by several of the men.

She approached and the young boy, she guessed to be no more than seven, who used her arrival, to flee.

Shawnee was now the only woman in the entire room, surrounded by mostly younger, well-dressed men. The dress she was wearing by itself would have stopped traffic. Her exceptional beauty however, was of no interest to these men. Over the exit door, she saw a rainbow flag and the few words WELCOME NAMBLA.

She could not escape that room soon enough-though none of the men paid her departure any attention.

An adjacent, large upstairs room had several tables around which were many of the major TV networks representatives as well as a few notable news anchors. This group was being addressed by George Soros and Ted Turner.

She heard Soros say, "In this time of fewer newspaper subscribers and shrinking advertisement dollars, we will maintain your businesses until the proper outcome is achieved by returning the rightful party to power. In return, each day, you will be advised which stories to report, which to spike, and what catch phrases to use. The public can not be allowed to think for themselves. We must use phrases that can be constantly repeated that an undereducated public will not question. In order for each newspaper or TV network to earn its money, each day a catch phrase will be provided. Any newspaper or media outlet NOT using the phrase or story line of the day will NOT, I repeat NOT get support money. Am I fully understood?" He was cheered by a standing ovation.

She flew out of that room into a pink room in which dozens of women were gathered. This time, every eye turned to look at Shawnee. She quickly served the food she had brought in but not before someone had felt her behind and another had slipped up behind her and kissed the nape of her neck.

She ran from that room escaping the laughter and cheers of the Gaia sisterhood.

Her last stop on the second floor was a room full of international guests-apparently from the United Nations. A Muslim cleric was addressing this entourage-

"We must defeat Israel and her proxies here- these evangelical Christians. Then and then only can our agenda, peace in the Middle-East, through the defeat of Israel be achieved."

That speaker was replaced by the vulnerable Walter Cronkite- "One world –that is the only way to achieve peace- the days of nation states are over."

Shawnee's head was spinning- every fiber of her being-all that she considered to be right and natural was under attack under this one roof. She walked toward the second floor porch-to try to clear her head.

She took in the view of the ERWACHE landscape that the Krauses had made for themselves. The moon rising in the east illuminated the zeppelin port while casting a romantic glow off of the lake at the foot of the castle.

She heard laughter and splashing. Peaking around the corner of the porch, she saw 3 topless women in a hot tub with Bill Clinton. The Ex-President was smoking a long cigar and laughing when he spied Shawnee, motioning for her to join them.

Again, she fled, as rapidly as she could- only to run right into Dr. Jo himself, who at this point of the evening was having great difficulty walking in a straight line.

"Ah, and what have we here?" he puzzled. "You look very familiar-have we slept together before?"

Too stunned for words, she just shook her head vigorously.

"With that body-how did I miss you? But I *have* seen you"...he reflected.

"I'm Tim's wife," she managed to say.

"Tim? Tim who?"

"Your worker-Tim McGregor- you know, the man you and Ingrid adopted and who lost his eye to one of your falcons."

"Oh, yes. Pity."

"Pardon?"

"Pity he isn't here. Come with me, I have something to show you."

Against her better judgment, she followed ERWACHE's founder into an upstairs office.

Inside the office were all kinds of books and framed documents.

"I believe you were told that tonight you would get information about that house where that haggard old skeleton was living. Well, here it is. The house is yours- free, clear- here is the deed, and you will see that all legalities have been taken care of."

This was too much to take in. After all these months, the hardships and disappointments, finally Aunt Mae's house was theirs. Here in the midst of all this debauchery and hedonism, the silver lining to a very big cloud.

"I don't know what to say- thank you so very much, I am just speechless."

"That's what I was hoping you'd say- now in appreciation- remove your dress," he said holding the deed temptingly.

Even as the words still resonated, the phone rang. With the unexpected phone call, Dr. Jo spilled his drink on his desk. The brief diversion was just what she needed to flee, tightly clutching the deed to Mae's.

Along with the deed a pamphlet, *Phoenix- Ein Neau Genesis-* something in German she guessed, was stuck. She rolled the papers up and fled. As she descended the stairs, she heard the grandfather clock strike 11:00. 'How to hide-how to hide-just one more hour'.

She glanced out at the front drive. Numerous rented limos were taking the special guests to the Krause's newly completed ski lodges for the night.

She worked her way toward the kitchen, hoping to hide there with busy work for the last hour. She washed dishes and pretended to be all about cleaning up though officially that was not what she had been hired to do... As she took the trash to the compactor at the rear of the kitchen- she encountered the mute serving boy she had seen upstairs earlier.

He was silently weeping. He could not tell her why, but when he stood, she noticed bloodstains on the back of his pants. She moved to comfort him but he ran off into the night.

She thought to herself- Lord Jesus- protect me. Please help that little boy.

It was obvious that the partying was going to continue at the ski lodges and no one would notice her leaving if she slipped out the back way.

She picked up the house phone and told Tim to pick her up at Lot 1 in 20 minutes.

She tiptoed from the kitchen toward the back exit- but that required her to pass the grand ballroom. There a small orchestra was playing "*Deutschland Uber Alles*" as every glass was raised in honor to... 'OUR LEADER'.

There at the front of the meeting hall was Dr. Jo with his glass in hand. From Shawnee's perspective, she thought that he was being saluted. She did not see him turn and salute with everyone else the huge portrait that had just been revealed.

The night air was cool and she got quickly chilled on her way to Lot 1. She hadn't gone 50 yards from the castle when she was overtaken by a security guard on a segway.

"You will return to the castle immediately."

"I will not. You can call Mrs. Krause – she hired me until midnight. Check your watch."

"Remain still. I will confirm your status."

The guard called via radio-
"Yes, she was detected in the area just outside the castle grounds. She claims to have been hired to work for Ingrid Krause. Can you verify?"
Voice over the radio: "Stand clear of the suspect. Affirmative. Escort that person to Lot 1."

Chapter 24

No sleep. Not one drop. She had had nothing to eat or drink, not even coffee. Still sleep was impossible.

All Tim could get out of her was that she was physically all right, though from her demeanor she was obviously traumatized during that night.

Sunday morning would usually be a joyous time for her as she prepared to go to church. She sat starring at the fire- mindlessly stroking Goodness and Mercy with an occasional pat for Grayboy.

She would not eat or drink. She simply sat and starred.

Tim was beside himself with worry. He decided to give Don and Martha a call. They were just leaving the parsonage when he reached them. Yes, they would be glad to come over. Two o'clock was decided on. Tim knew that for her to miss church, he needed to get her help and soon.

He finally got her to take ½ of one of his pain pills and she slept for 5 hours straight. Just after 1:15, he awakened her and all she could do was cry. She held him tight and wept.

He told her that the Trumbels were coming and she briefly went into panic mode until she saw that Tim had already straightened up.

True to their word, the pastor and his wife got there at the stroke of two. They came with Barbeque from Colleen and Shawnee's favorite- a malted grape milk shake. Pastor Don blessed the meal and everyone dug in, though Shawnee ate little.

Little was said as everyone ate.

Martha began slowly, "Shawnee, can you talk about last night at all?"

No response. Not so much as eye contact.

"This is what I was telling you over the phone," said Tim loudly. "She just sits and stares."

"This is a spiritual battle," declared Don Trumbel. "Her spirit has been so hurt, traumatized, that she may not speak without more help than we can provide."

"Do you mean taking her to a shrink?" Tim proposed.

"No. Join hands with us and let's pray for her right now."

The 3 joined hands and Pastor Trumbel prayed:

"Lord Jesus, your word tells us that where 2 or more are gathered in your name- there will you be also. We ask you to move in Shawnee's spirit- that those demons that so traumatized her spirit be bound along with father of all lies, Satan, and that Shawnee's tongue be loosed to your Glory. We pray these things not for anything that we would gain but that you Lord Jesus be glorified.

Please help her to know that she is loved with an undying love and that whatever power of evil she has witnessed, Our God is able to defeat it. We ask all this in Jesus' Name. Amen."

Shawnee grabbed all 3 of those in prayer for her and hugged them hard for several minutes. Each of the 3 spoke soothing words to her and then suddenly she started shaking. She wept briefly and then said to each, I LOVE YOU.

Gradually over the next 2 hours, she replayed every detail of the events of April 20th's party. Martha took notes.

The sun was low in the Virginia sky by the time she finished.

At the conclusion, she showed them the deed for the first time. Everyone was stunned, then saddened by the events surrounding the deed. Still if the deed was legal, at least some good had come out of all this.

"I found this too. I think its German- maybe some part of ERWACHE's plans-anyway I need to get it translated-this time by somebody trustworthy."

"I think it says PHOENIX- a New Beginning or Genesis," Pastor Don offered.

"Maybe put that away some place safe. Do you have a safe deposit box?" asked Martha.

Both of the McGregors shook their heads.

"How about under Grayboy's bed- until we can get someone to translate it?" Tim suggested.

"Sounds good-maybe I can get somebody at LU to help us," Don said.

Martha suggested a trip to help clear the air.

"Let's go to Bedford tomorrow- Peaks of Otter- our treat- how about it? Maybe we can take that memo or whatever it is with us and get it looked at."

"Wow, look at the time. Say dies anybody *need* an ice cream cone?" the Pastor asked.

"Actually no one needs one," Martha teased, "but my "All-American Teddy Bear wants one- anyone care to join us? Bring Grayboy and the kittens-let's all go!"

They piled into the Trumbels' van aiming to hit McDonald's before it closed. They spent a quiet 30 minutes eating ice cream on the lawn of McDonald's playing with the kittens and Grayboy. Below them, the occasional traffic on Route 29 passed heading north and south into the night.

Meanwhile, inside the gray work van, a balding man and a handsome man who had recorded most of the last 2 ½ hours conversation were particularly interested in the new German document. Things were beginning to fall into place. Just as soon as the families and pets left, the two shadows emerged and headed toward the back of the McGregor house. Once again, letting themselves in, they headed toward what they guessed was Grayboy's bed.

"Quickly- we don't have much time. "

"2 pages!? Look at this – this is a gold mine!"
"Make sure you get clear photos-but be quick- we don't know if they're coming back or how soon."
"Done-let's go."

The morning of April 22 was cool and breezy. The Trumbels picked up their friends at 10:00. Martha drove as Pastor Don told some of his football stories. He included an occasional jab at his wife who kept him grounded by reminding him just who had been first team All-American and who had not. Theirs was a friendly rivalry- steeped in love. The big red head driving was a sweet spirit but also a fierce competitor. She offset nicely the big teddy-bear demeanor of linebacker Don.
They spent the day at the Peaks of Otter and the National D-Day memorial in Bedford.
Tim said, "Now I understand that old veteran at your church. What incredible sacrifices were made to win for us our freedom? Those poor Bedford Boys and their families."
"Can you imagine dying for someone else?" asked Martha, winking at Don.
Tim could see it coming- now all 3 of them would start again about salvation. He led Shawnee up the path out of earshot of the Trumbels and just held her tight. He thought about never being able to hold her again. Eternal separation. He was shaking and not because it was cold.
She just held him drawing from him affirmation that she was loved.
On their way back to Lovingston, they passed the new LaHaye building at Liberty University.
"Isn't that a huge building!" commented Shawnee.
"All of the money for that building was given to Liberty by that writer, Tim LaHaye- the co author of the Left Behind series."
"Left Behind?"-Tim asked.
Pastor Don began slowly. "In the Bible, the book of Revelation describes what will happen at the end of the world. There will be a time when all those who have not accepted Jesus as Lord of their life will be left here in a time of total chaos. The believers

will be taken to heaven while all hell breaks out and breaks loose on earth."

"Theologians, those who study the Bible, call this the rapture" added Shawnee. "You know if you had listened to the Charlie Daniels CDs I got you for Christmas you would have at least have the basics on the rapture"-she said poking him in the ribs,

"That word doesn't appear in the text, but anyone who is 'left behind' will wish they had been raptured. Crime will be everywhere and everyone will be out to get whatever they can. Kind of a dog-eat-dog world, with no hope of law and order" added Martha.

"Until the Anti-Christ who will bring about false peace," Don added.

Tim was impressed that each of them understood each other enough that they could finish one another's sentences.

"So what about the people who are raptured? What happens to them?"

"They will go to heaven and be safe with Jesus forever"-Don concluded.

The minivan was suddenly cut off by a green pick-up truck whose rear bumper and back window were covered by obscene decals.

Martha swerved to miss the truck and everyone held their breath as she slowed safely.

"That could have been the end right there- Thank you Jesus and of course- thank you dear for that exceptional effort."

"We All-Americans are always ready," she teased.

"Could we stop to get some Advil," Tim asked. "My head is hurting and well... my eye is aching."

"Certainly. Wal-Mart ok?"

"That would be fine," Shawnee agreed.

As they got out of the minivan, Don pulled Martha close and whispered, "I don't think he'll be able to work-at least any time soon. We are going to have to be strong for them-they both may lose their jobs."

"Jehovah jireh, God will provide," she affirmed.

They walked arm in arm toward the Wal-mart entrance.

As the Trumbels and McGregors passed through the entrance together, the nagging beep, beep, beep of the metal detector went off.

"Whoops, sorry-forgot my cell phone," said Martha as she reached to turn it off.

The couples did not often get to *"Wally World"* so the trip got longer as they kept remembering things they needed.

Tim was feeling very weak so he asked Shawnee to walk him to the van. She left her cart with Martha and promised to return shortly.

As she and Tim exited the store, the incessant beep, beep, beep, of the metal detector went off.

Associate Brian approached the couple and since neither had any merchandise said, "It's probably just your cell phone."

"But we..."she started to say but Tim interrupted.

"Probably, thanks..."

"But Timmy we don't ..."

"I know but I feel so bad and those things always go off. Please help me get to the van."

She did and he promised he would be ok.

She headed back to the Wal-mart entrance and once again, the alarm went off. This time 2 security guards scanned her and nothing triggered the detector until one by accident passed by her head.

Beep, Beep Beep, Beep .

"Ma'am, do you have a plate in your head?"

"What kind of question is that?" asked the other, "go on in ma'am, some people's body chemistry just sets these things off."

As they were about to leave Lynchburg, Don suggested dropping off a copy of the Phoenix note at Professor Reynolds's office.

"He's a specialist in geopolitical studies."

"I guess that would be fine,"Shawnee answered, "but can we make it quick- Tim is really feeling bad."

"Sure- Martha my dear, pull in here – I won't be a minute. I do have to make a copy then I'll run it by his office."

A minute became 25.

When he returned, Tim was mercifully asleep in Shawnee's lap.

"I'm sorry it took so long- I couldn't find a working copy machine. Then when I did get the copy finished, Professor Reynolds was not in his office. So I had to leave it in his mailbox. I thought it would be a good idea to put it in an envelope-, which I did not have and enclose a note on paper I could not find. So, again sorry for the wait."

"It's ok, Tim fell asleep and I think that's the best thing for him."

Unknown to Pastor Trumbel or the others, it would weeks- not hours before Professor Reynolds would get the envelope. Earlier that same day he had been in a traffic accident, run off the road by a green pickup truck- and spent the next 2 weeks in Intensive Care.

2 weeks later, Shawnee and Tim sat and figured out their expenses. Tim's job was still open for him to return to but until he did, no money was coming in. When the call came from Ingrid asking if Shawnee could work at the Den for the next 2 weekends, her first inclination was to say absolutely not. But after further thought, the fact that Ingrid and Dr.Jo would be overseas for the next 2 weeks, plus their financial crisis, got Shawnee to agree to keep the place open.

The fact that soon they could set up a new home at Mae's and yet the reality that it was going to take money and a lot of it, got Tim to broach the subject of selling the truck to get cash for the both living expenses and the new home.

"Then what would we drive-the VW? No, I'm not going to allow you to sell your pride and joy. That would be like selling Grayboy."

"You are my pride and joy," Tim affirmed- holding her and kissing her repeatedly.

Her mock protests ended up in giggles as he tickled her.

"Seriously, we need to get some money together and those pseudo-doctors at the infirmary certainly aren't saying anything about you returning to work."

"I could sell my bass boat and trailer, maybe even the old fishing and hunting gear."

"Don't take this the wrong way but I was wondering if you, we, could sell the 32 Chevy. I really like it but it may be a long while before we can finish it and it might just..."

"Harold Finley."

Her puzzled expression let him know he had caught her off guard.

"Harold Finley is one of the pilots of the zeppelins. He told me if I ever wanted to sell the Chevy to let him know. I haven't seen him for awhile, not since the last work I did on it —maybe he would buy it."

"Why don't you ride over to see him tomorrow- it's a short drive and getting out will do you good."

"Agreed." They shook hands on it, kissed, then Tim turned out the light for the night.

Wednesday morning, Tim drove over to the zeppelin port. The few speaking workers and even a few of the mute ones, said hello or at least waved. He had taken to wearing an eye patch, much like those that pirates are traditionally shown with. Wherever he went , people instantly noticed him .He had begun to scan side to side more now that his field of vision was ½ what it had been.

He saw the pilot schedule and noted that Finley would be on duty the next 2 nights. Seeing that the shift would begin at 4 and it now being just after 11, Tim decided to check on the cars in Shaft 16.

From a distance, he had seen Rolf, but never got within shouting range. His mind was racing-if they'd let me get to some of those cars, I could restore some and sell the others and it would be clearing some junk out of ERWACHE's path plus we could make some money.

He entered shaft 16. From the lack of activity, it appeared the shaft had not had any traffic for quite some time.

He donned the required helmet and breathing gear, then settled in to the elevator car that took him hundreds of feet underground.

Finally, the eerie silence and almost total darkness of Shaft 16 and the auger that still lay there unredeemed.

He made his way through the adjoining tunnel, passing slowly along the line of cars. Yep, he had been right. The VW, a Maverick, it was a Fiat Spyder, then a Chevelle- maybe 1970,, a Dodge Scamp, a Ford Pick-up, a 1967 Mustang convertible, a Karmen-Ghia, an AMC Eagle wagon, a Buick Skylark and a Geo Metro Convertible. Each car looked to be in very good shape, though it appeared that the cars had hit each other-perhaps one at a time. In the limited amount of light that was given off by his lamp, he could not tell much about any of the cars-except they appeared to be in exceptional shape for having been in a coal mine.

He was admiring the Metro convertible when he noticed that the car was covered in more dust than the others- perhaps a small cave-in. He need to be careful –if there had been a cave in, a further one would leave him trapped and no one would miss him-since no one knew of his trip into this shaft.

Curiosity, not common sense, got the better of him and he cleared off the tail section of the Metro to see still another car- a yellow Jeep-the CJ type and in the fading lamplight still another – a red mini-SUV-that gay nudist's? Dust began to swirl and he realized just how easily he could be blinded-having now just the one eye.

He quickly retreated and exited the shaft. The elevator ride brought him back to the shaft entrance. He put his gear back in the ready room and headed out of the mine.

He glanced at his watch- it was now 3:15-"Wow"-he thought, 'that took a lot longer than I thought'. He headed toward the zeppelin port and caught up with Finley just as he entered.

"Tim, how are you getting on?"

"It's slow Harold- how are things in the wild blue yonder?"

"We're working more and enjoying it less. Say what brings you out here anyway?"

"Well, I remember that you said if I ever wanted to sell the '32, you might be interested. Well we kind of need the money and..."

"Baby coming?"

Tim paused, then simply said, "No, it's our first house."

"Sure, I'm interested in it- that is a classic body style- look I'm here for just 4 hours tonight- getting prepped for a big shipment for tomorrow night. Any chance that I could get a look at it tonight say around 8?"

Tim hesitated. Tonight was Wednesday and that meant he should join Shawnee at Bible study-but here was a chance to make some money-so without much thought, he said, "Sure, that'll give me some time to inflate the tires and clean it up some."

"Good- see you 8-ish."

He was very excited until he saw Shawnee's face fall when he said he was not going to the Bible study. She said she understood but he felt like he had let her down-again.

True to his word, Harold arrived at 8:15 and the 2 men examined the '32 for over an hour.

They were still talking when Shawnee got back Tye River.

Harold stopped to admire her-and simply said now he understood why Tim wanted to please her.

"So what's a good price?"

They haggled for a few minutes then Harold made a final offer- "tell you what, you once told me you'd like to ride in the zeppelin sometime- how about this- $8,000 and a trip tomorrow night?"

"I thought that ERWACHE forbids such trips-didn't you tell me that once? I don't want you to lose your job over a balloon ride."

"Well, you know, the Krauses are overseas- what they don't know won't hurt them. So how about it? Bring the wife, if you want to. There is plenty of room and she'll enjoy it I'm sure," he said secretly thinking how nice she would be to look at for the otherwise boring ride.

"The price is fine- and at least 1 of us will meet you at the LZ at 6:45 tomorrow-sound ok?"

"Deal. Oh, and drive the car over tomorrow night —I'll load it on my trailer when we get back."

Chapter 25

The next evening, Harold was somewhat disappointed when Tim and Don met him at the LZ.

"Harold this is Don, Don —Harold. My wife did not want to come but she thought that the trip might be good for me. I hope you don't mind."

"Not at all. We just don't need you to board until the TODTs are all aligned. So you can watch us for a few minutes and then I'll give you the high sign —just climb to the cabin platform and we'll be off to Norfolk."

In all the years that Tim had worked for ERWACHE, he had never been this close to the entire zeppelin operation-it was fascinating.

Just after 7:30, the massive ship _Weisel_ lifted off from it's mooring and slowly ascended to the cruising altitude just above 1500 feet. The sun was just setting and the view was magnificent. There was just enough light in the woodland below to see deer and turkeys and at least one fox. Don and Tim were staring at the ground but soon the darkness swallowed the wildlife below. In the not far distance, there were brilliant arc lights. As they approached Charlottesville, it was obvious that the lights were coming from some U Va. function.

"Probably spring football or lacrosse," shouted Harold over the roar of the Daimler engines.

"My bet would be football," said Don.

"How close to the interstate can we fly?" asked Tim.

"We have to stay south of the highway until we get over Fluvanna. From there until we reach Short Pump, we can fly along the shoulder. At about Short Pump, we have to climb to 4000 feet so as to not get the world below upset. We will stay at that altitude until about Hampton. Then gradually we will descend. The entire flight takes about 1 hour, depending on the wind currents."

The nothingness of the counties of Fluvanna, Goochland, Louisa, and Hanover passed rapidly under the great ship.

Cars below on the interstate were completely oblivious to the vessel and crew above them.

"What's tonight cargo?" inquired Don.

"The usual. Two coal TODTS and the middle one is pork renderings. A pork TODT is not nearly as heavy as a coal one so we flank the pork with the heavier TODTs to help with stability.

We will unload the coal TODTs first and simultaneously. Then we will head toward the open ocean, a couple miles off shore or so, then drop the pork. On the return trip we will pick up –let's see" –he studied his manifest, "looks like a TODT full of antique cars, some live pigs, and some heavy equipment."

"Those antique cars would be right down your alley Tim" –Don offered.

"So might the heavy equipment. Is that mining equipment?" Tim asked.

"Could be. The Krauses are always bringing new stuff in. Might be for the ski slope set up."

"What are those lights?" Tim pointed.

"That's the baseball field- the Diamond where the Triple A Richmond Braves play, farm team for the Atlanta Braves."

"Back to the pork drop."

"Yeah?"

"Is that legal? Doesn't EPA or some government agency control that? How do the ..."

"Krauses get around it? They know people *and* they have deep pockets."

The giant ship continued on past Richmond International Airport.

"How about airspace- how do you know how high to fly?"

"The FAA has total control- that's one agency we have to obey. We usually fly north of the field."

East of the airport, the lower lands of eastern Virginia led to the Williamsburg -Yorktown region. The absence of large population centers relegated the crew to watching traffic until suddenly the lights of Hampton, Newport News and Portsmouth exploded beneath them. The coal terminal lay just ahead to the southeast.

Tim and Don watched with rapt attention as the zeppelin dropped the outside TODTs and yet the ship remained very stable.

As the coal TODTs were being attended to by the ground crew, the *Weisel's* Daimler engines roared to life and off they flew toward the ocean.

Over the ocean but well within sight of the coast, slowly the ship turned. The ship suddenly lurched upward, tossing Tim and Don for a loop.

"Updraft!" shouted Harold.

When calm returned, Tim found himself to be somewhat sick at his stomach. Heading toward the restroom in the corner of the ship's cabin, he glanced out the porthole at the ocean below. Illuminated briefly by the ship's lights was a sea of red. Tim struggled with his good eye to see what was in the water below. There seemed to be activity in the water- maybe sharks? What with all the pork renderings that had been dumped, it seemed logical that the sharks would congregate for a free meal.

Pastor Don had recovered from the updraft enough to gaze out a second porthole and catch some of the activity below. What he saw caused him to doubt his own eyes. The *"updraft"* had really been the sudden release of the tons of unwanted pork byproducts. Or was it only pork? He thought that he would ask

Harold about what he had seen but something told him that Harold was less than honest-maybe trying to hide something. The ship returned to the coal port, dropped off the empty TODT then gingerly maneuvered into a new alignment. As the wind picked up, the massive Daimlers helped to stabilize the ship. Those on the loading dock secured the enormous cables that held the TODTs in place.

Pastor Don glanced at his watch and noted that the entire transaction had taken just under ½ hour. ERWACHE had always prided itself on efficiency and he had seen it now first hand.

He was about to call Martha on his cell phone when Harold asked him not to.

"It interferes with the air to ground link up. Sorry."

"Not at all. Was that updraft just coincidental as you were dumping back there?"

No answer. Don tried again, this time watching Harold carefully. He knew that Harold had heard him but he also knew that Harold was not answering. He looked at Tim, who had just rejoined them coming out of the bathroom.

"You ok?" asked Harold.

"Ok, now. Say back there I saw something peculiar..."

Just then the great ship lurched downward- effectively ending all thought and most conversation.

"Hold on! Rough weather ahead."

A short storm of relatively low intensity cast the ship and crew off course for the better part of 1 hour. The Daimlers strained, gradually pulling them out of the storm.

Once they were west of Richmond, the storm was just a memory, albeit a bad one.

They were now over Louisa County watching the sporadic traffic below on Interstate 64.

"Look at that car- it's got to be going 120 or more," Don observed.

" 132 to be exact"-corrected Harold. "Watch this."

Harold flipped open a tube like pointer, pressed a button and the speeding car came to a sudden halt.

"What is that gadget?" inquired Tim.

"Nifty, huh?"

"What is it?"

"It's a miniature EMP gun. Electro- Magnetic Pulse gun. It's something that the Krauses got from the Department of Commerce during the Clinton years."

"I'd think that something like that wouldn't be under the Commerce Department-seems more like a weapon," Don posed.

"You didn't hear it from me but the scuttlebutt is that some of the defense department's top secrets got sold to anyone with money. The Clinton's got lots of weapons put under the Commerce Department then it was open to the highest bidders. The Chinese got some of our top missile technology for the right price and the Krauses got this toy for a few dollars more. By the way, that person driving is Martin Jensen of 192 Old Chimney Road, Scottsdale, Arizona, as he read the print out from the gun. We will be sending his violation to the Virginia State Police for a share of the fine."

"Share of the fine?"

"Yes. We have a deal worked out. Mark Warner cut a deal with the Krauses."

"The governor of Virginia?"

"Former governor. Remember those signs on the interstate-SPEED MONITORED BY AIRCRAFT?"

Both visitors nodded.

"That's us." Serving humanity."

"What about his car-what happened to it?"

"We fried his computer. You know the US can do the same thing from outer space?"

"Really?"

"Yep. Welcome to the future."

If the zeppelin trip was out of the ordinary, both Tim and Don would not have liked what was going on back in Lovingston.

Shawnee had gone to the CVS to shop for a few necessities. As she approached the checkout counter, she saw Megan talking with 2 well-dressed men. The men were so intensely interrogating Megan that they did not notice Shawnee behind them.

"Well, here she is, ask her yourselves," Megan pleaded.

Somewhat chagrined at their inattention, both men instantly turned and glared at Shawnee.

"Ask me what? Who are you and what do want from me?"

"Forgive our rudeness, Mrs. McGregor," began the handsome man.

"We are with the government and we need to ask you some questions about your aunt."

"She passed away last fall"...

"Yes, we know, please accept our condolences," said the balding man.

"I'm sure that she paid her taxes- that's it isn't it. You must be from the Internal Revenue Service. I can't tell you..."

"Ma'am, we aren't IRS. Is there somewhere we can talk-more privately?"

Megan interrupted-"Shawnee- can I talk to you a minute?"

Shawnee nodded and moved toward Megan.

"My daddy told me to always be careful of strangers, even if they are from the government- my uncle Ted said *especially* if they are from the government- course he was a moonshiner," Megan whispered.

Shawnee agreed for once with Megan's father's advice.

"What should I do-Tim's away for the evening, what should I do? - she whispered back.

"Why not go over to the Subway sandwich place- if you really are going to go with them. I can watch you from here and make sure that you are safe. They already told me that they know where you live- so you can't go home."

"If they weren't from the government, I'd lose them driving Tim's truck- ok, but when you get off can you come right over and rescue me?"

"Sure- I'll be off in..."

"Ma'am, I hate to interrupt but the clock is ticking- you know- the government hates to pay overtime. We won't keep you very long-we just have a few questions to ask," the handsome one said.

The poise and ease with which he addressed the women caused their fears to subside.

Even so, it was not without great hesitation that Shawnee and the 2 federal agents headed toward the Subway. She was somewhat comforted by Megan's pledge and she was constantly looking over at the shop- keeping her promise.

Shawnee wasn't hungry though since the 2 agents offered to buy her something, she opted for a Diet Coke. She also picked a table well within Megan's view and somewhat away from the door.

"Just what part of the government are you with," she inquired.

"Homeland Security"-quickly offered the handsome agent.

"You might say Homeland Security but it's tied to veteran's affairs as well," corrected the heavier, balding agent, now fervently digging into a meatball sub.

She studied the men. Neither had said grace. Both were well dressed but the bald one wore a tie while the white chest hairs of the other agent stuck out of his unbuttoned collar. Who are these guys really she thought?

"What do you know about your aunt's life before she came to the USA?" asked the hairy chest, now working over a turkey club sub.

She recounted the little that she knew. Both men pursued their meals as they had not eaten in days.

"I had a book that had some of her life story in it I think ..."

"You had?" both men asked at once.

She studied them. Both had pounced. Why?

"Yes, I had this book- in some foreign language and"...

"Then you don't have the book any longer?"

"I gave it to my husband since his boss was going to get it translated and it got lost."

"His boss-that would be ..."

184

"Dr. Krause. Dr. Josef M. Krause-the owner of ERWACHE. We thought he could get it translated for us- and actually, he did. Or at least said he did- Oh, I don't know – The book got lost while he had it. The one thing I do know –Dr. Krause said that my Aunt Mae left us the house. It was in the book."

Neither agent said anything but looked at each other.

"There's something you aren't telling me isn't there?"she implored. "What is it? The house does belong to us doesn't it-I mean – Dr. Krause got us the deed in our names- it's legally ours isn't..."

"We don't know- we don't have an answer."

"Have you noticed any peculiar things happening at ERWACHE?" the bald one asked.

"I'll say. Where do I begin? I could start with..."

"Shawnee! What are you doing here? Are the boys back from Norfolk? Don said he was going to call me from the blimp but he hasn't yet."

It was Martha.

They hugged and Shawnee began to introduce the agents then realized that she did not know either of their names.

"These are 2 government agents- investigating some things about my Aunt Mae."

"Oh, what agency are you with?"

"Homeland Security and Veteran's Bureau," Shawnee answered.

That's a peculiar combination Martha thought to herself. Why here? Why tonight? Government agents working beyond office hours? She pulled Shawnee aside.

"Did you see any identification?"

"Well, no but I think they're ok."

"Shawnee let's at least wait until the boys get back. These guys may seem ok but something this important –I think our guys should hear with us."

As the girls whispered, the 2 *agents* spoke briefly.

"Did you hear that? The men are on 1 of those flights right now. Finally a break-let's not spook them- let's excuse ourselves and leave."

"Shawnee! Are you doing ok?" It was Megan keeping her promise. Suddenly the small sandwich shop seemed crowded. The agents arose in unison and said their good-byes. "If you need to contact us, Mrs. McGregor- please call this number- 24/7. Again we have some more information to share on your aunt." They nodded toward the table full of women and left.

Shawnee introduced Megan to Martha and the 3 sat for a few minutes, watching as the agents left.

"I can't thank both of you enough. I didn't feel real comfortable with those 2. Thanks to both of you."

"Megan, I'm the preacher's wife over at Tye River. We'd love to have you come visit some..."

"Thanks but no thanks, my folks said that that church has a bad a reputation. We know the Davenports real well and they said that church is being run by fanatics."

Knowing that Shawnee might respond, Martha quickly said, "Well if you ever change your mind- the door is always open."

"If everything is ok here, I think I'll get home-got a government test to study for."

They said goodbye to her.

"How did you stay so calm after what she said?"

"No, matter what they say about Don- I know his heart and so do you. Megan may come around later-but at this point she's convinced that she knows the truth, Better to part as friends-at least for now."

"Let's head back to the house. The guys should be getting back sometime soon."

Somewhat worse for the wear, airship *Weisel was* docking at the LZ.

As Harold Finley guided the ship into dock, the 2 visiting passengers were allowed to watch the TODT's being detached and the anchoring lines being set next to the other 2 zeppelins in port.

Within minutes, the crew except for Finley, Don and Tim had all left.

"Great flight. Thanks." said Don.

"Yeah, we enjoyed it. Want to load up the car now?"

"I'll have to do it. The area where my trailer is is restricted. You two can stay here while I test drive it and then load it."

"Test drive it?"

"Yep. Figured I had better see what I'm paying 8 grand for. You can hang out in the shop while I'm gone."

With that, he left them in the huge restoration shop.

The first TODT was being automatically delivered to the restoration area on giant rail tracks. Suddenly one end opened and the cargo was revealed. Both men were awed by the variety of old cars and trucks. While they watched this marvel of automation, nature called Don.

"Where's the bathroom?"

They both looked around. There didn't seem like there was a restroom anywhere. Don discovered an old style grease pit-the kind where the mechanic went down some steps to stand under the car while he serviced it. Don walked down. At one end of the pit was a door with a sign- but not in English. He tried the handle but it was locked.

"Watch out!" Tim shouted as the second TODT from tonight's cargo was heading toward the pit. Don was not in danger of being hit but possibly getting stuck under it. He scrambled up and out with time to spare.

Both men watched as the TODT came to rest over exactly where he had been. This was a bottom loader as opposed to TODT #1-the one full of cars. According to Harold this one was full of pigs.

It was impossible to see what was happening as the TODT came to rest and began to unload.

"This is weird- pigs into a grease pit!"

"Who knows?" Tim offered.

"Hey, you guys ready to go?" It was Harold. "I just got a warning from the guard. I have to go now. Better come along."

As they turned to leave, TODT #2 began to move back toward the LZ.

Glancing over his shoulder, Don noticed that the pit was empty- no trace of pigs- not even the smell of pigs. He did see something that he had not seen in his brief search for a restroom. A small doll.

The 3 men headed toward the newly loaded 1932 Chevy. Harold was 15 to 20 paces ahead when a security guard approached, shining his flashlight at Harold.

"You are leaving, correct?"

"That's correct."

The guard just as abruptly turned and left.

It's like we aren't even here Don thought. The guard did not even acknowledge our presence. And those pigs. How did they get through a locked door?

Chapter 26

April was ending. Despite the promise Shawnee had made to keep the Lobo's Den open, since May 1 *was* a company holiday she did not feel bad about keeping the doors shut the next day either.

Tim was ordered to report to the infirmary in 2 weeks for a physical and despite his fragile condition, if he was deemed able to work, he would be working the following week. But at the moment, another weekend was upon them. They spent Saturday with the Trumbels scrapping paint off of the house that soon they would occupy. There was a running conversation between the friends about all the strange events that recently occurred. Meanwhile their conversation was at least partially being recorded. Grayboy, safely distanced away from the kittens, sat close by.

"Just who do you think those government agents really were?" posed Don.

"I don't think they were who they said were. They did ask me if we ever saw anything strange at ERWACHE. I told them that I had but never got to elaborate. I've seen so much. Really, where should I start? How about how they seem always to find us. Coincidence? Or how about that horrible night at Castle Krause? Or the other one at Lobo's Den? Or the "doctors" who took care of Tim? Or their whole pagan set-up?"-Shawnee posed.

"I took notes the day after that April 20th party, remember? Well, I've done some research. You remember Shawnee, about that room with the big rainbow and the WELCOME NAMBLA sign?

Shawnee paled. She said nothing but nodded.

"Maybe we need to talk about something else." Don offered.

"No, its ok, I'm ok," Shawnee finally vowed.

"You sure?" asked Tim.

"I'm ok, what does NAMBLA stand for?"

"Don, I don't know if I should," she looked imploringly at her husband.

"Tim, Shawnee, Martha discovered that NAMBLA is the abbreviation for the North American Man Boy Love Association."

"Does that mean what I think it means?" Tim asked.

"Their motto is 'Sex before Eight or its Too Late'. Have you ever heard anything sicker," Martha asked.

Shawnee was even paler than before. "So that explains that poor little boy in the kitchen," she finally said.

Everyone was silent for a few minutes.

"If that kind of stuff was going on, that's totally illegal- you know sexual abuse of a minor-how could anyone possible get away with that stuff?" asked Tim.

"Liberal activist judges and political correctness" answered Don. "You see since the Supreme Court refused to take a stand on pornography in 1974, each community gets to set its own standards of what it right and what is wrong. Reason was stood on its head. From a Pastor's perspective America basically told God that they don't need Him, His Word or His Son."

"It's obvious from everything that Shawnee saw that night and the other episodes at the den, that are some really strange things going on, but whether they are illegal- I don't think we could prove anything without lots of proof," said Martha.

"*Yet.*"

Everyone turned toward Shawnee.

"I know that this may cost us our jobs but there are just too many things about ERWACHE that need to be investigated."

"But by whom? The agents that you met? The FBI? The local police? And for what?" Tim asked. "If we aren't careful we will lose everything that I,... we have worked for."

"Still there are a whole lot of abnormal things going on-like the zeppelins dumping pig remains in the ocean that Tim and I saw- I just can't see how they can get away with that. And the speed monitoring system on the highways. I guess the Virginia state government could let them do that but it just doesn't seem right."

"No one can explain away that "art" in the den's upstairs. That was just perverted."

"What everyone here is missing is that the Krauses do a lot of good things," Tim countered. "Look at the jobs that they create for local people and for the disabled."

Shawnee could feel her temperature rising. She counted to 10 before answering.

"Timmy, remember they could not have been colder toward us last October when we lost Mae and the baby. And with your eye- they never once looked in on you-the very people who "rescued" you from Woodrow Wilson. Both of them have come on to both of us- that Dr.Jo gives me the creeps. Ingrid could not be much colder. I'm telling you that they are evil."

"Evil is a really strong word. I told you that they were very precise people and probably more German than American."

"Still the way they treat us and everyone else- they just have total contempt for everyone who isn't just like them."

"Well, at the risk of offending you three- do you, as Christians, hold non-Christians in contempt?"

The trio of believers looked at each other.

"Tim, none of us is perfect or righteous- none of us. We *are* different because we trust Jesus as our Lord. Lots of people hate His name because He called each of us to decide whether to accept Him or not. Those who don't trust Jesus believe that they can make it through life on their own- without any accountability- they, in effect, – become their own gods. Now do we hold others in contempt? No. We are not high and mighty but the One that we serve is. He wants everyone to accept the free gift He gave to any who will receive it."

"Free gift?"

"Salvation. Being eternally with Him in Heaven. You see all this world has will pass away."

Martha chimed in. "Like this paint, Tim. It wasn't always faded and cracked was it? Once it was fresh, bright and shiny. But like this paint, our life on this earth is not permanent. You like country music right?"

He nodded.

"There are a couple of country songs that I know you have heard."

"Like?"

"This World is Not My Home, I'm Just Passing Through or Will the Circle Be Unbroken?"

"I 've heard the second one."

"When they sing 'There's a better home awaiting, in the sky Lord, in the sky,' what do you think they're singing about?"

"I don't know- I guess I never really paid much attention to the words."

She continued. "Tim, we just want you to know that Jesus loves you and everyone. People have to be willing to choose Him. He could have made all of us puppets-but he gave us a free will. Some people will turn their backs on Him —like the Krauses-because they are sold out to a lifestyle that says that this is all there is. It's the 'what's *in it for me lifestyle'*."

"It's Satan's lifestyle," added Shawnee.

"Come on! Satan? Is he for real?" Tim asked.

"YES!" All three Christians said in unison.

"Is that in the Bible?" Tim demanded.

"It most certainly is. There are many passages about who he is, what he tries to do to us and how he can disguise himself in very seductive ways," Pastor Don said.

Silence set in for a few moments as they watched Goodness and Mercy chase Grayboy away.

"Alright," Tim said at length. He figured that everyone wanted to have him accept Jesus but in his heart he still was not sure. Grayboy circled back and sat at Shawnee's feet-having lost the kittens.

"I'll tell you what. I've always wondered about what goes on out there after dark- let's go see if we can find any evidence. But I think everything is on the up and up."

"Even finding the cars of 2 people who disappeared in that shaft? That's normal?" Shawnee fired at him.

Tim had forgotten about that. "Are we sure that those 2 cars are the same ones that those people drove- remember I only had a brief look with 1 eye. Maybe I could slip back in and..."

"No, I don't trust those people- I think the 4 of us should go snoop around- some night after dark." Shawnee proclaimed.

"And look for?" Tim demanded. There is no way that the mine will be accessible after dark."

"How about that grease pit?"

"Grease pit?"

"Where we saw the TODT deliver pigs to a closed door."

"I think that if we go, we would have to cover a lot of ground from what I've seen of the layout." Martha added.

"Layout? You sound like a professional criminal." Pastor Don teased. "Did you case the joint?"

"Let's just say that any good team needs to know the strengths and weaknesses of their opponents. We first team All-Americans know that." She teased back.

"One thing that Martha said is right. We would have to know what we are looking for. Maybe 2 of us could probe the pit while the other 2 ..."

"Checkout the TODT"s- see if there really are pigs in them."

"Well, I'm not wise-but if we get caught we could be charged with trespassing. How are we going to explain *any* of us being there?" Tim wondered.

"How about this," Shawnee offered. " We ride on 4 segways over toward the LZ. Maybe Martha and I could say that we were walking the tram tracks for exercise while you two look around?"

"My little outlaw," Tim grinned.

"We need to know the zeppelin schedule and wait for a moonless night," she concluded.

"It would help if there was diversion- like another party," Martha suggested.

"The road race!" Tim almost screamed.

The others looked on in silence-waiting.

"Each May, third week of May, Dr. Jo sponsors the Peaks of Otter hill climb for all of his rich car racing buddies. They race Friday and Saturday during the day and then come back here for a huge party."

"Not another one- I know I can't take another one of those parties", Shawnee lamented.

Pastor Don put in- "How about Friday night of the race week end?"

"I think Thursday night might be better," Tim suggested.

"Why?"

"They all clear out beginning Wednesday afternoon- that would give us extra time if we need it."

"Ok, everyone in agreement then?"

Back on Front Street in Lovingston, the agents were elated by what they had just heard. The gray work van had been manned by one or the other one of them since they met with Shawnee.

Later that night, just before going to bed and after saying prayers, Pastor Don confided to Martha, "I think we may be in over our heads. What if those people are doing something horrific? I think we should go to the authorities and not go snooping."

"I think we shouldn't snoop but... well, I think Shawnee senses something in her spirit. ERWACHE may just be a peculiar company run by Bohemian eccentrics. Yet, what if she has uncovered that horrific something you just mentioned? Maybe we should get some outside help but from whom and about what?"

"Earlier today," he said, pulling her close, "you said that a good team prepares by knowing its opponent's characteristics. What do we really know about ERWACHE? Besides doing a generic word search on the Internet, we need to know more about their whole operation. I wonder if Dr. Reynolds ever translated that memo we left. "

" Yeah, funny how we didn't hear from him."

"He's real busy- maybe even out of the country- remember he goes to Israel several times a year."

"Well even if this just a bunch of liberal Germans, I'd feel better and I know Shawnee would. I am afraid that Tim isn't onboard with us –but at least he's more open to the gospel- I think."

"Good night, my hero."

"Good night, Pastor."

Chapter 27

In the days running up to race weekend, the couples spent more time together firming up their goals. In reality, they did not know what they were looking for. They had not actually seen anything illegal-at least from the corporation, just suspect behavior from ERWACHE's founder and his wife.

Race week saw a flurry of activity – all employees were encouraged but not required to attend the races. Since Dr. Jo always expected to win, he liked having a "home-town" rooting section-even if some of the employees couldn't root.

It was obvious that to carry out an adequate investigation, the couples needed to split up to cover as much of the facility as possible. They met on Tuesday night and Wednesday morning at the McGregors discussing strategies. The kittens and Grayboy dozed peacefully nearby.

"Ok, the weather forecast is calling for chance of showers, so now what?" asked Don.

"Well, if it does rain, will all those people be headed back here?

"Tim, you're the only one who can answer that – what have they done in years past?" asked his wife.

"The corporation rents the Peaks of Otter Inn and all the motel rooms around Bedford for Thursday and Friday nights, come what may. We should be ok all night Friday if we need it."

"Everyone has 2 flashlights and their walkie- talkie –complete with spare batteries, right?" asked Martha.

Everyone checked and nodded.

"Ok, so Martha and I are going to lag behind you 2 at the tram entrance at the Lobo's Den. Once you get to the auto shop, you 2 are going to flash a signal to us."

"That's assuming that we make it to the auto shop"-Don interjected.

"I really think we can make it. The few staff that are left behind usually has their own party."

"How do you know so much about it-personal experience?" Shawnee teasingly demanded.

"So I was told," he said sheepishly.

"Let's say it's raining cats and dogs," Don posed- "we will need to coordinate our watches."

"This is sounding more like a World War I over the top operation"-Martha stated.

"Let's hope we have more luck than any of those poor soldiers," Tim countered.

"We can't trust in luck- we need to turn this whole thing over to the Lord."

"Amen to that," confirmed Shawnee.

"Back to the operation, in the off chance that we have trouble, Shawnee and I will need to divert the attention of any guards doing their duty. How about a small brush fire- about the time that you 2 enter the shop?"

"The flares that I bought can be lit in the rain so if you 2 could start a small fire, there shouldn't be any real problems- the underbrush is dry but not so dry that there will any real danger."

"What about the cameras- are they fully charged and do you both know how to use them," asked Shawnee.

"I've been practicing- got lots of pictures of the most beautiful girl in the world," Don vowed.

"You've been taking pictures of Shawnee?" Tim demanded.

Shawnee blushed. "Timmy stop that – you know he meant Martha."

At 4 pm, the couples drove to Colleen for burgers and milkshakes.

"We might as well have one last good meal before tomorrow's adventure" suggested Don Trumbel.

"You did say good, didn't you?" Martha played.

"Sure- ice cream and burgers- sounds fine to me, huh, Tim?"

"Yeah. Sure." Tim answered. He had been very quiet and it seemed that of all the "investigators", he was least enthusiastic. His quiet was not lost on Shawnee. She so wanted to prove that the Krauses were up to no good but she also knew that Tim had really mixed feelings.

They sat out along the retaining wall beside the old drive-in and watched the traffic on Route 29.

"We need to be going," Martha reminded Pastor Don. "The Hymn sing starts in 40 minutes. Will you two join us?"

The McGregors looked at each other, neither answering.

"Give us a few minutes, ok?" Shawnee began then just as abruptly said, "No actually y'all go on ahead. We need to talk."

Handshakes and hugs were exchanged and the Trumbels drove away.

"Ok, Timmy, what's up?"

"The usual. Plus I'm having really cold feet about tomorrow night. I don't think we should carry out the plan."

"Oh. I guess that all we suffered over the last 6 months isn't that important."

"Of course it's important. It's just what if we get fired and lose everything?"

"Yep. What if? We would still have each other, the pets, a house, and 2 very close friends. Many people don't ever have those things."

"But what have the Krauses ever done that..."

She began to tear up and then through broken tones said, "They hurt you. They have insulted me and you - as a family. They are just evil people. They ..." she couldn't continue.

He held her close until she regained her composure.

"Please drive me to Tye River. I need to be in the service tonight."

The trip was in total silence. He pulled the truck up to the chapel and she was about to get out, when she implored one last time,

"Timmy, won't you please come in with me?"

"I can't ... I just can't ... not yet."

She shrugged and walked away.

He switched off the truck and sat in silence thinking about disappointing his wife, losing his job, and how empty he felt. The night was warm and the moon was low yet, hidden by the mountains. He glanced around, his gaze coming to rest on the grave of their daughter. Sliding down from the truck's seat, he walked over toward it. In the quiet, he heard the crickets, Martha at the piano, and the singing emanating from the open church window:

> *On Christ the solid rock I stand,*
> *All other ground is sinking sand,*
> *All other ground is sinking sand.*

He looked at the small tombstone of the daughter they had never seen. He felt a terrible weight in his heart. Could his daughter have been saved some how? Singing voices once again interrupted his thoughts...

> *"What a friend we have in Jesus,*
> *All our sins and griefs to bear!*
> *'What a privilege to carry,*
> *Everything to God in prayer!*
> *O what peace we often forfeit,*
> *O what needless pain we bear,*
> *All because we do not carry,*
> *Everything to God in prayer!'*

Tim began to tear up. He started to pray to a God that he could never relate to prior to this moment.

"Please God; help me to know what to do. I am so confused. I just want justice. And comfort." The words interrupted again...

> *'Can we find a friend so faithful?*
> *Who will all our sorrows share?*
> *Jesus knows our every weakness,*
> *Take it to the Lord in prayer!'*

Tim looked around. There was no one in sight but he felt that he was not alone. A small rabbit sat 20 feet away munching on grass.

The night was very still and Tim was suddenly better.

He looked again at the small stone and at the stones of Shawnee's parents and her aunt. He thought about having never met his in laws but how exceptional they must have been to have raised such a daughter. In-laws and a child now together-but according to Pastor Don- he, Tim, would be separated from them forever. Separation from Shawnee- he could not stand the thought...

> *'Softly and tenderly Jesus is calling,*
> *Calling for you and for me;*
> *See, on the portals He's waiting and watching,*
> *Watching for you and for me.*
> *Come home, Come home,*
> *Ye, who are weary, come home;*
> *Earnestly, tenderly Jesus is calling,*
> *Calling o sinner, come home!*

Slowly Tim walked toward the Tye River church. He couldn't... yes he could...why should he... there was plenty of time...No there wasn't – no man knows what tomorrow holds...you can wait... no you can't ....the struggle between his ears was once again interrupted...

> *'I will a-rise and go to Jesus,*
> *He will embrace me in His arms,*
> *In the arms of my dear Savior,*
> *Oh there are ten thousand charms.'*

He slipped and nearly fell. Tears were streaming. He was sure that he should go in but strangely, his hand would not grasp the doorknob. With both hands, he turned the doorknob and the door swung open.

The only eyes that greeted him were Martha's. She began to play

'Safe in the arms of Jesus,
Safe on His gentle breast,
There by His love o'er-shaded,
Sweetly my soul shall rest...

She winked at Don. The Pastor arose and turned to embrace Tim.

"Tim, have you come for a reason tonight?"

Through choked off tears – Tim said- "I want Jesus. I have had no peace since that day that you were bitten by that snake-even before that – I don't know if Jesus will accept me but do you think he will?"

"I *know* He will."

"What do I say?"

"Do you love Him?-tell Him. Confess to Him your sins-and ask Him to save you. It's that simple"

Through choked off sobs, Tim accepted Jesus.

Shawnee and the small congregation embraced Tim. Martha played …

'Tis so sweet to trust in Jesus,
Just to take Him at his word
Just to rest to rest upon His promise
Just to know "Thus saith the Lord."
Jesus, Jesus Precious Jesus …

Pastor Don invited everyone to the small church kitchen for cookies and punch.

Shawnee had not let go of Tim's hand since he had come forward.

She was smiling in a way that he had not seen since their wedding day. She was more beautiful than she had ever been. They excused themselves from the impromptu reception and were about to leave-when he said one more thank you to the Trumbels.

"We didn't do anything that is special. You have made a decision that you will never regret."

"I just felt ...convicted...that Jesus gives you all so much peace- I wanted what you had. I have never felt as loved as I have right now. One more thing..."

"Yes?"

"More than anything, I want us to find out what is going on. I'm...make that we... are going to pray for success tomorrow night."

"Let's get a good night's rest and pray for good weather and that God will reveal to us what He wants us to know," Martha suggested.

Tim and Shawnee cuddled on the way home like the newlyweds they had every right to be. She kept squeezing his hand, without saying anything. From time to time, she kissed his hand.

"Let's see if there is anything good on the radio," he suggested.

"Tonight, I think I could almost listen to opera," she purred.

She turned the radio on to a punched his pre-set to the country station he loved.

As the distance home grew shorter, the song they heard had a new meaning for them,

> *Yeah, when I get where I'm going,*
> *There'll be only happy tears.*

Thursday, May 23rd, dawned rainy and cool. The town of Lovingston emptied slowly as the workers either traveled to Bedford or headed for parts unknown. Tension set in around noon, and got thicker as the afternoon lengthened. Naps were tried but to no avail. The weather cleared about 2 pm so the likelihood that the town would be repopulated, looked slim.

At the agreed upon time, the Trumbels drove to the McGregors. Don then followed Tim to Lot 1 where Tim left the truck. Back at the McGregors, the couples began to march toward Lobo's Den.

Just across from the den, Pastor Don got everyone into a final prayer huddle.

"Lord Jesus, we pray for safety. If there is something that needs to be revealed, we pray that you help us report what we see accurately and that in everything your name be exalted. Please forgive us for trespassing. Please show us the paths that we need to tread. In Jesus' name we ask it, Amen."

It was now dark- just after 8 pm. Don and Tim, walking counterclockwise rapidly, followed the tramline until they reached the shop according to plan. A last minute change- sending a short blast over their walkie-talkie- the men reported their success and the women began their task.

The auto-shop was easy to access- though it looked quite empty. The men waited outside the shop watching for the girls' signal- the small fire that was supposed to draw any security away from the men.

No one was prepared for what happened next.

Shawnee and Martha set their brush fire up in a very orderly fashion- making sure that a tall large fire would flourish but not spread.

As Martha and Shawnee stood admiring their work, but before they could light a match or strike the backup lighter, an extremely bright light emerged behind them.

Turning in unison, they beheld a gigantic fireball well behind them, beyond the mountain.

"Whoa, when those girls start a fire they don't play around," Tim observed from the ½ mile that separated them. "Let's go."

While the men entered the garage, the women were staggered by what they saw.

"The Lobo's Den! Oh, no. How could...?"

"It's too late to worry about that- let's make tracks!" Martha urged.

"But go where?"

"Let's stay as far as we can from the men- maybe head to toward the infirmary."

We can say we were walking along exercising, minding our own..."

Her sentence was cut off as two flashlights blinded her.

"You will come with us." The nameless, faceless guards addressed Shawnee only. Martha got the distinct impression that they neither saw her, nor were they interested in her. She thought about simply walking away but dared not leave Shawnee alone.

Meanwhile, 2 men were viewing the blaze at the Lobo's Den with admiration.

"If nothing else comes out of this investigation, we knicked them."

"The couples wanted a fire and they got one."

"Let's hope that the men have success."

Tim and Don were silently making their way toward the grease pit. There was no one in sight and the overhead lights were almost all off. The only appreciable light was a yellowish glow that came through the opaque glass of the door at the end of the grease pit.

As they climbed down into the pit, they noticed a symbol on the door for the first time.

"I've seen that before I think"- mused Don. "I just can't remember where."

They got to the door and pushed. Surprisingly it opened.

Once inside- they entered a large room- perhaps a receiving room.

There were 4 possible exits from that large room. The first exit looked to be a small 2 foot by 2 foot door that was hinged at the top-much like what a dog would use to enter and exit a house.

The other 3 doors were larger and more standard but progressively taller from left to right.

Door number 2 might have allowed a toddler or young child through it.

Door number 3 would probably accommodate a 4 ½ to 5 foot person.

The last door was a standard size 8 foot door.

Since both investigators were over 6 feet tall, the obvious choice was door 4.

"Let me photograph this before we go in"- Pastor Trumbel said.

Once on the other side of the fourth door, there was a peculiar odor- not readily identified but it permeated everything.

As they made their way down a long corridor, there were a series of rooms-each locked but in a special way-cell doors!

As they peered into the darkness of the first door- they heard movement. They turned their flashlights on an illuminated a 4 naked men. The men were all starring zombie-like at the flashlights.

Each man was completely naked. Each was extra-ordinarily blonde.

"Can we help you? Please tell us how to help you," Don pleaded quietly.

No response. The men appeared incapable of speech and made no gesture of acknowledgement.

Tim moved up the corridor- "Pastor!"

Tim had discovered another room this time 4 women, also naked and listless. No response to voices. All striking blondes.

The intruders made their way down the hall, unfortunately uncovering 40-50 rooms all in the same state as the first 2.

Toward the end of the corridor was a hallway that ran perpendicular to the one that they had just left.

Heading down this new hall there were 3 doors on their left and 4 hall ways on their right.

A quick check beyond the first left hand door revealed a corridor just like the first. Small rooms filled with possibly 10 to 14 year old boys and girls- all naked, all isolated by sex, none responsive to Tim or Don's voice.

"Pastor, I've seen enough," Tim said weakly.

"Me too."

They were about to reenter the connecting hallway when they heard footsteps. 8 large men all in ERWACHE jumpsuits were leading 4 naked women back to one of the *"rooms"* in the first hallway.

Tim and Don waited until the footsteps were no longer audible then went into the connecting hall. They stepped into the 3rd hallway only to see again rooms with cell doors and small children, 4 to a room, this time not segregated by sex. In each of these "rooms" regardless of age, there was no provision for sanitation.

The only bedding appeared to be mattresses thrown on the floor.

None of those imprisoned were responding to Tim or to Don, though all of the inmates did respond to light.

Having seen 3 of the 4 hallways, Don cautioned, "I'm not sure I can stand the last corridor. I think I know what's in there."

The men cautiously made their way into the common corridor then tiptoed toward the last door. Inside the last door, there were many small rooms that contained ...human body parts, not just human body parts –infant body parts. Rooms with literally thousands of aborted children were on either side of this last hallway.

As big as Donald Trumbel was, as many sports injuries as he had seen, he had never seen or dreamt of anything so vile. He got physically sick.

Tim was equally ill. It defied imagination what they were seeing.

The stunned men meekly made their way toward the connecting hall but froze again when the sound of footsteps were heard coming toward them.

With not a little panic, they looked at each other and got relief only when they realized that the footsteps had made a right turn down one of the unexplored hallways.

They waited for what seemed like an eternity, then poked their heads out of the corridor of dead infants.

"Let's get out of here!" Tim implored.

"But how, if we go back the way we came there may be some of those goons in the first hall we went through."

"There has to be a way out down one of these other halls-let's try the one closest to us".

"Lord Jesus- we need your help-please protect us and these poor people," Pastor Don intoned.

It was slow going down what proved to be a mostly unlit hallway.

From time to time their flashlights would reveal another atrocity against humanity. Children in all sorts of dismembered sections. Laboratories filled with human tissue and skinned carcasses.

Both men vomited again.

As they left that hall- they entered another perpendicular hall, this time much shorter-with 2 signs but neither said exit. As quickly as they could, they made tracks toward one but stopped abruptly.

"We didn't take any pictures beyond the first chamber. We have no proof except what we saw. We need to go back."

"Pastor, I can't."

"Then I will."

"No, I won't let you go by yourself".

They turned and headed toward the door that led to the hall way not yet traveled.

About halfway up the hall were four rooms adjacent to each other. As they got nearer, the sounds of a physical attack in progress was heard coming from the closest room.

Tim and then Don peered in to see what was going on. In this first room were 2 men raping a woman of about 25. She made no protest.

It took every ounce of strength that Tim had to restrain Pastor Trumbel-he pulled him quickly away, whispering,

"We can't help them. That woman and probably the others have been doped or something."

"I can't stand this. As God as my witness, those men will pay!"

"Pastor, let God repay them- we have to get out of here with proof or all this will have been wasted. Do you have your cell phone?"

"Yes, but I turned it off a long time ago. Why?"

"Can you take a picture or 2 without the flash?"

"Why sure- I see what you're saying."

Don Trumbel, all 6 foot 5 inches of him, slid quickly back toward the room and got 3 pictures.

With no hope of helping those being victimized, the 2 men headed toward the last 2 doors they had seen.

Opening one, their lights revealed a huge tank, full of rotting corpses. They both got sick again but there was nothing left to vomit. A vacuum line led to an upper chamber- possibly directly into a TODT.

The last door mercifully led to a staircase. A guard station was at the top of the stairs but again, mercifully, it was unmanned.

A small handwritten note was attached to the door,

"Boris, we are having a party with the new arrivals- some real lookers- join us in hall 6. Fresh meat."- Hans

Tim remembered to photograph the sign and the 2 men found their way back to Lot 1.

Neither man said anything. They stood silent for many minutes, then got into Tim's truck.

All the way back to the McGregor's, neither man spoke.

They were surprised to not find the girls. Worry set in.

"Do you think they are all right" Tim finally asked.

"No note or anything, pretty strange."

Don noticed the answering machine flashing and pushed the button.

"We are ok," it was Shawnee's voice. "We are at the sheriff's office. Please come get us when you get home."

There was a footrace to the truck as the investigators piled in, not knowing what to expect downtown.

Chapter 28

2:00 am, Friday morning. Tim's pickup slid into the small Nelson County Police Department lot. Hurrying toward the door, they were amazed to find that they had to produce photo id's to access the building.

Once inside, they were led to a large room where Shawnee and Martha were being questioned by a detective and by Rolf.

"Make them confess. They are the only possible suspects," demanded Rolf.

Detective Cochran, deftly, coolly, asked simply, "And you sir, if you are the second in command at ERWACHE, what am I to charge them with? There might be a possible trespassing fine but certainly not any jail time."

"Confess you two!" demanded Rolf. "You have caused me to miss half of the weekend having to deal with all this mischief. Confess now I say!" He rose menacingly and tried to get at the women.

Cochran was a very strong 6'7" tall and the most convincing of Nelson County's law enforcers. He said simply, "Sit down Fritz or Heinz or whatever your name is or I'll put my size 12 somewhere where it hurts. No one has been charged with anything. The fire marshal has to conduct an investigation."

"Confess to what?" Shawnee demanded.

"How dare you question *ME.?* I ought to beat you myself."

"You touch one hair on her head and you answer to me!"

Everyone turned to see Tim and Don entering the room.

"Look Cyclops, your wife burned down the Lobo's Den! She must be made to pay."

Tim and Don looked at the girls but said nothing.

Finally, Martha said, "We did not set fire to the Lobo's Den or anything else."

"You are lying!" screamed Rolf.

Pastor Don got up to protect his wife.

Rolf considered the size of the man protecting Martha and backed down.

Deputy Cochran spoke at last. "We have no grounds to hold you unless ERWACHE presses charges for trespassing."

"We most certainly will".

After paying the bond, the women were released to their husbands with the promise to reappear before the judge in 10 days.

"That was close-we could have been in jail over night at the very least," Martha said.

The 4 of them squeezed into Tim's truck, Martha having to sit on Don's lap.

"What were you 2 able to find out?" demanded Shawnee.

Both men were completely drained of energy and emotion. The thought that their wives would be charged with arson was the final emotional tumble that they did not need.

Neither man could bring himself to talk.

"What's wrong- we're ok, so how did it go?"

"Don? Tim? Why aren't you talking? Is it too crowded in here to talk?"

All Don could do was to hold his wife in his huge arms, shivering.

"Is Don ok?" Shawnee asked. "Timmy why aren't you 2 talking to us? Are you mad at us? We really didn't set that fire-we never even lit a match."

Silence.

Tim drove the truck quickly toward home. By the time the 4 arrived at the McGregors it was 4:45 am.

Still neither man had said anything. Shawnee opened the front door and all 4 entered.

Martha still holding Don tight, eased him toward the armchair so he could rest.

Shawnee put Tim to bed.

"What is going on? It's almost like they are in shock," Shawnee observed.

"You may be right on the money. I've never known my Don not to talk to me —even if I did make him angry- and I don't think that they are angry- they may not be able to tell us 'til later."

"Let's all nap until say 10 am. Maybe rest is the best medicine."

The Martha's cell phone went off at 6:45; it was Professor Reynolds at Liberty. She tried in hushed tones to communicate that he needed to call back later. The professor was adamant. He had to see them, all of them, immediately.

Martha rose and nudged Shawnee who had curled up at Tim's side.

"Boy, I hate to do this but Professor Reynolds at Liberty needs to meet with us immediately. He said it may be a matter of life or death!"

With that last word, Shawnee jumped up and together the 2 women woke their respective sleeping husbands.

"The fastest way is Tim's truck but we can't all fit in it and ride to Lynchburg. Let's pile into the VW and drive to the parsonage. We can take our mini-van from there."

Not without great effort were the 2 women able to get their groggy, strapping six footers into the cramped confines of Shawnee's bug.

Neither man was very conversant though there were a few short words exchanged.

They rode to Tye River, swapped cars then Martha drove while Shawnee did her best to help her stay awake. Don and Tim were asleep in the second and third seats.

The miles between Tye River and Liberty flew by, with Martha pulling into the pre-arranged meeting place the Lynchburg Howard Johnson's Restaurant, by 7:55.

The women did not awaken their husbands but instead went in together. Martha was fairly sure what the professor looked like even though she had never had a class under him.

"Mrs. Trumbel?" asked a tall graying man in an orange polo shirt.

"Professor Reynolds? This is Shawnee McGregor."

Handshakes and brief hellos almost instantly led to,

"Where are your husbands? This is urgent; we have no time to waste. I called off all of my classes today for this. Where are the men?"

"We had to let them sleep- they had a hard night- they are in the car, we'll go get them."

"Quickly- meet me in the conference room past the breakfast bar."

Never one to shun breakfast or any other meal, Pastor Don was waking up slowly until he walked by the food, then he appeared to have a new lease on life. Unfortunately, there was no time for food-as the couples made their way into the conference room while the professor drew the sliding wall closed.

"Why all the cloak and dagger?" asked Martha, "Why did you say that our lives may be in danger?"

With that, the sliding screen opened and in strode 2 men, both vaguely familiar to Martha but instantly recognized by Shawnee.

"What's going on? Why are these 2 men here?"

"Who are these 2?" asked Don and Tim almost simultaneously.

"Allow me to introduce Agent Urias and Agent Rosenberg, with Israeli intelligence and Simon Wiesenthal Institute."

Don and Tim were just now beginning to become lucid.

"Pardon me, Professor Reynolds, what do these men want from us?" Don asked.

"We want to save your lives," professed the balding agent.

The two couples starred at the agents as Professor Reynolds began.

"You have stumbled into something that will be difficult to understand and even more difficult to explain. I have ordered coffee, lots of it, and some pastries to try to sustain us over the next few hours."

"Hours?" asked Tim-"just what is going on."

"Agents Urias and Rosenberg will have to do most of the talking, although everyone is free to ask questions and seek explanations. Is everyone in agreement?" Professor Reynolds begged.

All nodded assent but Pastor Don implored that whatever they discussed be covered in prayer. He rose, albeit unsteadily and said,

"Oh God, our Father, help us to bear what we hear and reveal what we have seen in ways that will glorify our Lord and Savior Jesus Christ, Amen."

The Israeli agents did not say amen but had bowed with everyone else.

Agent Urias rose and began to speak slowly.

"I don't believe anyone in this room, any of the 7 of us has the full picture of what is going on at ERWACHE. We have perhaps together, enough information to call for a federal investigation but we will not know until each of us has had a chance to contribute."

He walked toward the window and leaned against it now facing everyone at the table.

"I need to start with Maria Ludlov, Shawnee's Aunt Mae. It is her story that begins to unravel what has been built here in the Virginia Mountains. Maria Ludlov was one of twins. She and her identical twin sister Anna were born in Lithuania in 1930. They were blond and blue eyed- indeed those of you who knew her, she still had those beautiful eyes even in her later years. But she also carried with her an awful story and a hideous tattoo."

Tim raised his hand asked, "Is that what we discovered the day she died, the 1409-2 on her forearm?" Nodding in agreement Agent Saul Urias continued.

"At age 13 ½ , they were taken by Hitler's Nazis to one of the most notorious of the concentration camps, Auschwitz. There they became guinea pigs for some of the most diabolical "doctors" that the world has ever known. These so called doctors were fascinated by what Hitler had proclaimed the Master Race-the blonde, blue eyed Nordic stock that Hitler himself could never have qualified for. They took it upon themselves to mass produce babies of this description throughout World War II." He stopped to take a sip of coffee.

"If I may interject," Professor Reynolds said, "this was the Lebensborn program. It started with 'pure blooded Aryans'- by Hitler's definition, being bred with other 'pure-blooded Aryans'. This actually became like horse breeding, with 'stud farms' being set up."

Saul Urias concurred.

"Even with all the emphasis on mass producing babies of the 'correct racial heritage', the number of babies that Hitler was demanding was far above what could be delivered. So, the Nazi's began to experiment-with people of the 'correct' appearance."

At that moment, Shawnee arose and slipped her ERWACHE windbreaker off, silently folding it but not before Agent Urias said, "Thank you."

"Thank you for? Taking off my windbreaker?"

Agent Uri Rosenberg spoke for the first time. "Mrs. McGregor, these people that you have been working for have been hiding for years in plain sight."

Everyone was unsure of what he meant.

"Perhaps I may help," the professor offered. "That innocuous jacket holds a clue to just what we are dealing with. Please hold it up so that everyone may see the ERWACHE symbol.

She did so and the professor continued- "that symbol which adorns the nose of all their zeppelins, is that of the Waffen SS, those who conducted the experiments on Aunt Mae and thousands of others."

There was silence for a moment, then Pastor Don asked, "Is that the reason for the night flights?"

"Partially, there was the fear of traffic accidents from onlookers, but it was because of their "business" that they also flew at night," added Agent Rosenberg.

"Their business?" asked Martha, "We supposed that it was coal and pigs."

"That is what everyone has been led to believe, but let Agent Urias take us further."

"Let's start with the company name, ERWACHE. In German, this means AWAKE. It was one of the main themes of Nazi Germany- to awake its citizens to the threat of 'lesser beings'. Unfortunately, ERWACHE today has become synonymous with kidnapping and cloning."

Chapter 29

"Kidnapping and cloning? Someone explain that please!" begged Shawnee.

"If I may, let me go again back to the story of Maria and her sister. The Nazi 'doctors' began to seek ways to produce the numbers of babies, racially correct babies that Hitler wanted. So they gathered sets of identical twins to experiment with- especially 'Aryan' or 'Aryan looking twins'," explained Saul.

"At Auschwitz, the Waffan SS was gathered to experiment with children especially twins. Inside Auschwitz, a Doctor Wirth oversaw that part of the camp, but he gave free reign to Doctors Mengele, Clauburg and Schumann. Those 3 were allowed to torture, maim or experiment with the children in any way that the 3rd Reich would benefit. One of them ordered the repeated raping of Anna and Maria Ludlov by 'Aryans'. These little girls were virgins when they were captured but were raped by hundreds of the Nazi 'supermen' over the course of 3 years. The girls were made pregnant but then had their pregnancies terminated in the 3rd or 4th month through needle extraction. Eventually, their pregnancies were terminated at 2 to 3 months by the same method."

"Is that what happened to my baby?" Shawnee sobbed.

Silence. What could anyone say?

As Tim tried to comfort her, Saul continued

"We have only just confirmed this story since last October. Maria Ludlov's diary is our source."
"Her diary? Shawnee demanded." What diary? Was that the ..."
"Little blue book written in that beautiful foreign language? Yes."
"But how did you get it? It's been lost?"

Agent Uri Rosenberg now rose and made a confession, "We, the people of Israel, owe you an apology. We have been tracking World War II Nazi war criminals for decades. Sometimes we get real lucky. Your aunt was a fine woman who suffered for not just her family but for all freedom loving people everywhere. What they did to her was so horrible that the world should not forget. We, took it upon ourselves to photocopy your book."
"When? How? I don't understand."
Agent Urias, took over.
"Do you remember the night of your aunt's death?"
Shawnee nodded.
"The dog was inside with her when the health worker left, yet it was tied up outside when help came later. We had staked out your aunt's home, we had a tip that ERWACHE knew she had something on them, and that she might testify against them.
"The wedding! No wonder the Krauses would barely acknowledge her, they must have seen the ..." her voice trailed off.
"Tattoo? -that is our thought as well. We had her house staked out the night she died. Unfortunately someone slipped past us and apparently tranquilized the dog."
"But what for?" Tim asked. "She could barely speak at the end."
"Her book- that Shawnee already had, they came looking for it and may have killed her."
"Was there an autopsy done?" Professor Reynolds asked.
Heads shook asserting none had occurred.
"May we now apologize again for what we did?" asked Uri.
"What did you do," demanded Shawnee.

"We planted a listening device on the dog's collar and then over the next few months waited until we could slip in and copy the book."

"Why of all the nerve-you probably heard all of our conversations –even the private ones!" Tim exploded.

"Again, we apologize. We heard only the conversations that took place when the dog was close by. We destroyed any embarrassing, to you, conversations, but we were running out of options. With the death of the main witness, our only hope was that we could discover from the book what she had seen." Tim cooled off.

"One more thing, I'm sorry to report that your Aunt Mae did not leave you the house."

"But we have clear title," argued Tim.

"That may be, now, but it was a ploy to buy your loyalty. ERWACHE is a rich and powerful company. I'm sure Dr. Josef M. Krause is capable of buying lots of things."

Shawnee was ghostly pale. Everyone was starring at her as she tried to speak. Finally –

"Doctor Jo's middle name is Mangle- I saw it the night that I got the deed. It was on his college diploma."

More silence.

Professor Reynolds broke the silence. "I've been working on a theory. I will need Tim and Shawnee's help. What are the dates of your company's holidays again?"

Tim rattled off the litany of unusual company holidays.

"January 20th, March 7th, March 16th, April 20th, May 1st, July 4th, September 4th, September 14, September 28th, October 7th, October 29th, and December 25th."

Working furiously at his laptop for a few moments, he startled nearly everyone when he announced:

"If indeed this is an extension of Nazism into the 21st century, maybe these dates will be of interest. I don't find any major birth dates for January 20th so let's come back to that one.

I did find that March 7th is the birth date of Reinhold Heydrich, who was named to become Hitler's heir but was assassinated.

March 16th is the birth date of Doctor Josef Mengele the so-called Angel of Death at Auschwitz. He was the one most often associated with the experiments on twins. He escaped to South America and basically got away with murder.

April 20th should be the biggest party of all if this theory holds true, that is Adolf Hitler's birth date."

Shawnee virtually leapt from her seat, "That explains all that evil that I saw at the 'castle' that night!" She fell into Tim's arms too exasperated to speak.

Martha spoke again, "I took notes on what she said and heard. There were all kinds of bizarre groups and weird agendas being honored that night, like NAMBLA."

"We know. The paper that was stuck to Shawnee's deed, *ERWACHE EIN NEAU GENESIS* has given us a wealth of information, we , uh, we copied it one night while you all eating at McDonald's ."

"That's not possible," Tim asserted. "We always lock the house.!"

Holding up a small pry bar, Agent Urias continued. "We had to. These people do not play. We wanted to catch them but protect you as well."

"Listen here's more," commented the Professor who had been working hard on his theory.

"May 1st, besides being an international socialist holiday, is the birth date of Dr.Horst Schumann, who was in charge of sterilization at Auschwitz.

July 4th, has me stumped. I don't find any connection to the Nazis."

"There may not be one," Tim offered. "In all the years that I have been at ERWACHE, we have never celebrated Independence Day-Never. No fireworks, nothing special-just a day off- like any Saturday."

"September 4th," continued Dr.Reynolds, "Dr. Edward Wirth-born this date- overseer of Auschwitz. He gave the green light to use children as guinea pigs.

September 14th- I do not find a connection with the Nazi's.

However, September 28th, is the birth date of Dr. Carl Clausburg, head of the insemination unit at Auschwitz. The infamous Block 10."

Furiously, Pastor Trumbel scribbled down this information.

"October 7th, Heinrich Himmler's birth date, he was the overseer of all the death camps. A former chicken farmer and a battered husband-hardly anyone worth emulating-he committed suicide rather than be tried for war crimes.

October 29th, let's see. Josef Goebbels birth date- he was Hitler's mouthpiece and propaganda ace. A club footed midget-hardly an Aryan.

That leaves us with December 25th, which should be..."

"But isn't, celebrated" Shawnee shot. "It's like the fourth of July- a token holiday to not draw attention to them."

"Well what does all this add up to?" posed Dr.Reynolds. "We have here a company that seems to venerate dead Nazis but I don't know even if an autopsy was done on Maria Ludlov, that we could prove anything."

"I haven't said much but I have something to add that may be of interest," volunteered Don Trumbel.

"One of those days that you thought I was sleeping in class," he said looking at Dr. Reynolds, "I heard something that is pertinent to this whole story. January 20th is the anniversary of the Roe v. Wade case-that made abortion legal in America. Let's play a hunch- look up Margaret Sanger's birthday-see if it's the missing September 14[th.] Is it her birthday?"

"It is," concurred Dr. Reynolds.

"You know what is significant about her?" He added." She is the one who said that Hitler had it right. That the strong should abort the weak, that poor people should be sterilized. She also advocated racially cleansing by doing away with black babies. From our work with National Right to Life, we found out that most of the abortion clinics here in the USA are in predominately black neighborhoods."

"So do we have anything that would bring a conviction on anything?" asked Martha.

"Yes-_we_ do." It was Pastor Don looking at Tim. He held up a symbol he had sketched.

"Waffen SS-Leibstandarte", identified Dr. Reynolds.

"We have been into the pit of hell itself. Tim and I were inside Block 10 last night."

Chapter 30

"That explains why you both were tongue-tied last night. We thought that our arrest was the cause." Shawnee volunteered.

"Arrest?" puzzled Dr.Reynolds.

"We got blamed for setting the Lobo's Den on fire-not that it hasn't crossed my mind lots of times, but we didn't do it", Shawnee added.

"Say would Israeli intelligence have had any interest in burning down the den?" she asked pointedly.

"We," Uri began, looking at Saul for approval- "let's just say, let's just say we needed you to be successful last night."

"Every one stop for a moment. The Lobo's Den – if we translate that to pig-gin German it becomes the Wolf's Lair, Hitler's hide out in East Prussia."

"Still that is not enough to file charges. What did you two see last night?" asked Dr. Reynolds.

Slowly, methodically the story began with the trip to Norfolk on the airship Weisel.

"Horst Weisel was a Nazi hero- a song commemorating him was popular throughout Germany during the war. Another coincidence?" asked Dr. Reynolds.

"Perhaps," continued Don. "We flew to Norfolk and watched as they unloaded the TODT's."

"Todts- did you say todts?" asked the agents together.

"Yes, Topographically Oriented Delivery Transports. They are the containers that are hung under the zeppelins..."

"That may be, but todt in German means death. The SS wore a special Death's head insignia," exclaimed Uri. "These people are *so bold*; they must think everyone is stupid."

Don continued. "We flew to Norfolk and turned around over the ocean as they dropped pig renderings..."he stopped and choked.

"What is the matter?" asked Martha. "Don, what's wrong?"

Tim continued for Don- "Until last night we thought that ERWACHE was dropping pig renderings- they aren't, they are dropping human body parts. Parts that they are harvesting from people being held below the auto shop in some of the old mine shafts."

"People being kept in mine shafts? Is that what you saw?" Saul asked.

"Not really in mine shafts," Don said rallying. "They have an elaborate system of tunnels and rooms. We saw people being raped, people being left stretched out for experimentation, and containers full of human body parts. I took a few pictures but I think that they are inconclusive."

He passed the cell phone around and everyone grudgingly agreed that the pictures were of little use.

"And you didn't tell the police or try to help?" asked Martha.

"He did try to help but I restrained him," Tim said. "There was nothing that we could do- they keep the prisoners doped – everyone is naked-even the children. It's the most horrible thing..." he lost his voice.

"And since we were suspected of arson-you couldn't very well tell the police. I'll bet that Detective Cochran would take the case-he's hardnosed and no nonsense, but"...Martha added.

Everyone was silent.

Finally, proof. The eyewitness accounts of 2 people. This was more than enough to bring about an investigation but how and how soon.

"We aren't dealing with small timers-this is the big leagues-we need to get to the FBI as soon as possible," Dr. Reynolds stated.

Everyone pondered what their course should be.

Finally, Saul suggested, "It is now just after 1 pm. It is Friday afternoon and the ERWACHE races will have their attention for at least another 24 hours. If you leave now, could you gather up your belongings enough to meet a helicopter in Charlottesville by 5:30? I believe that the Israeli government will give you refuge long enough to get the proper investigation begun."

"All of us?" Tim asked.

"Certainly- we are like your Marines-leave no one behind."

"Professor- what do you think our course should be?" Don asked.

"There are really only 2 witnesses; you both need to be safe. Despite all that we have discussed, if you two are lost, there is no case."

"Why don't Shawnee and I go get the things we will need and meet you in Charlottesville?" asked Martha.

"I don't like that idea- not after I saw the look on Rolf's face at the police station," said Tim. "I've never seen him so mad."

"Let's do this- we 4 will do as Saul has suggested. Saul and Uri do what you can to arrange the transportation and Dr. Reynolds..."

"I will first pray for all of you then call the FBI and see if I can get the ball rolling."

"Now everyone remember that we are dealing with desperate people who are no respecters of human life," Uri reminded.

"Meet us in the UVA "pregnant clam" parking lot at 5:30." "Any questions?" Saul asked.

"I still don't understand the cloning part," Shawnee expressed.

"That's for another time —when we put this bunch out of business,"Dr. Reynolds offered.

"One more thing," Pastor Don said as he formed everyone into a huddle for prayer.

"Lord, you have shown us in your word that 7 is the number of completion. We 7 here, we need help in bringing this evil down. We ask protection for everyone here and that you be glorified in Jesus' name, Amen.

Good-bye and Shaloms were exchanged and they went their separate ways.

Chapter 31

"So let me get this straight- my aunt was being raped for her pre-born babies to provide-what?"

"Cells to produce super babies- the Nazis got very close to cloning people. Think about making copies of people- carbon copies of people-how weird is that?" Tim asked.

"From what I've read, they got real close to doing it," Martha said.

"So what's with it today?" Shawnee implored.

"There are people that believe using embryonic stems cells will cure everything. It's basically a justification for abortion- and has become a big black market. Some of the really rich are reputed to be getting stem cell injections from aborted children," Pastor Don narrated.

"Why?" asked Shawnee.

"Vanity," Martha chimed in. "There is a belief that those cells cause the aging process to stop and even turn backwards."

"So it all comes down to money." Tim advanced.

"Not just money- the love of money being the root of all things evil. Its man's fallen nature-sin that has caused this. Though the love of the money and the pride of life are enmeshed as well."

They rode on in silence- thinking about what had to happen in the next few hours.

Don Trumbel pulled the mini-van into the Colleen Drive-in for what might be their last visit for a long time. As they sat and ate in the van, he reminded everyone to just act naturally when they got back to Lovingston. The town should be virtually empty, with the race being held in Bedford.

"I think it would be best if we all went to your house first," Martha suggested. "I know it doesn't make sense in the scheme of things, but I still believe that there is strength in numbers. We can help you load quickly and then backtrack to Tye River then finally up 29. In fact, we don't really have to go to Tye River at all, the quicker we are out of here the better for all of us, I think."

They voted and Martha's plan won.

They pulled into Lovingston just before 4 pm. The house was just as they had left it and Grayboy greeted them happily from the back yard. Inside, the day to day struggles of Goodness and Mercy seemed to have continued unabated. Shawnee let Grayboy in and he licked everyone then began his usual pursuit of safety from the *yellow peril.*

In a few minutes the McGregors had all that they thought that they might need. Tim had pointedly shown Shawnee that his Bible was packed into his suitcase. Their few possessions from the not yet year that they had been married were easy to sort through. A few pictures, a few odd trinkets, nothing of great importance.

"Should I bring this ERWACHE pamphlet that's under Grayboy's bed?" she asked Tim.

"Good idea. Let's put him outside-he'll be ok and the cats too."

As the McGregors secured their pets, a rumbling was heard, and it seemed to come closer. Grayboy bristled and barked as 2 ERWACHE uniformed guards dismounted from their motorcycles, right in front of the house.

Tim was certain that he had never seen them before. The guards had not seen Tim or Shawnee-both having ducked as the sound approached.

Tall and handsome, these guards looked like Nazi storm troopers, thought Don Trumbel as he let them in. Both men looked coolly around the room. Both were armed. The Trumbels were on either side of the men, facing them.

"Tim McGregor? Mr. and Mrs. Timothy McGregor?" asked the first officer, who stood closest to Don and almost eye-to-eye, height- wise.

Don and Martha shook their heads. "We are not the McGregors."

"We are!" Tim called as he and Shawnee entered the house from the rear.

"You will come with us."

"What on your motorcycles? Why? Why should we go anywhere with you?"

"A car is on its way. You will join us. The Krauses wish to see you. It is urgent."

"I'll bet it is," Tim said as he partially lunged at the men, but tripped and fell.

The second officer drew his gun and pointed it menacingly at Tim.

"Now you will come with us."

"*Coastal Carolina!*," shouted Don Trumbel.

Without another word, Martha Trumbel , 24-year-old Martha Trumbel , former All-Big South and First Team All American mid-fielder, Pastor Don Trumbel's pride and joy, soccer tackled the man closest to her. The gun went flying. The man fell hard into the door jamb-head first.

At that same instant, Pastor Donald Trumbel, former All Big South and Second –Team All American linebacker- Donald "Rumble" Trumbel, put "his hat in the numbers" for the first time since his playing days at Liberty. He smashed into the first officer's chest –using his helmet-less head as a weapon.

The sudden blow- close to the solar plexus left the first officer out cold.

Tim and Shawnee were amazed. Here were their 2 closest friends, their Pastor and his wife on the offensive.

"That was pure Goldberg, Pastor!" Tim said as he assisted the Trumbels in tying and gagging the guards.

"Goldberg?" Shawnee quizzed.

"Zidane. Goldberg. I'll tell you later."

Pastor Don surveyed the 2 downed guards.

"Quick- you 2 have got to get out of here," he proclaimed.

"We all need to get out of here," Shawnee corrected.

"They aren't looking for us –they want you two."

"Hurry- we can outrun them in the truck," Tim suggested.

"I think they will be looking for the truck- take our van. We'll still meet you at 5:30, Lord willing," Pastor Don coached.

"But we can't just leave you!" Shawnee was pleading. "Please come with us!"

"Just go- we will be fine- they want you not us. Now go please!"

Everyone hugged and the McGregors sped away in the Trumbel's minivan.

"Jesus, keep them safe," Pastor Don prayed.

"Come on Pastor-let's hurry."

Out the backdoor sprinted the Trumbel's . They got to the end of the yard just as two green sedans screeched to a halt in front. Don quickly but carefully hopped the fence as Martha eased Grayboy over. Then she hopped it as well.

They slipped quickly into the wooded ravine behind the house toward the river.

Meanwhile, throughout Lovingston, all engine noise ceased. The McGregor house was completely awash with security people inside of 10 minutes.

At the same time, Tim and Shawnee were traveling rapidly north on 29 just outside of Covesville, when the van sputtered and shut off.

"What the dickens...?"

"Out of gas?"

"No-it just quit."

"We are almost insight of Mae's, should we..."

Her question was drowned out by the sound of a helicopter.

Their hope of a quick rescue was dashed by the sight of the copter's now all too familiar ERWACHE logo.

The chopper landed and an unsmiling Rolf, gun in hand waved them into the craft. It soon disappeared into the Virginia twilight.

Back in Lovingston, all traffic except ERWACHE machines were stopped for inspection. The police, being immobilized, had to rely on ERWACHE for information.

All entrances and exits to Lovingston were covered and sealed off by ERWACHE, they *thought*. Helicopters, blimps, motorcycles, car, trucks, segways were all being used to conduct the search.

If the ERWACHE security force had really been on its toes they might have seen a man and his wife calmly paddling downstream, with their dog, in a wooden canoe.

"Lord, forgive us for taking this canoe. Please help Tim and Shawnee. Help us to repay evil with good. If we have wronged any man save for the owner of this canoe, please do not hold it against us. Help us to repay the owner for his loss. Amen."

"Coastal Carolina!?!! I never thought we'd ever need that in our entire lives," she said stroking Grayboy.

"That was the game of your life and it established your reputation as a head hunter. That's what led to you becoming an All American. Thank God you remembered, you may have just made the play of our lives."

They paddled steadily in the growing darkness. No one pursued them but they also did not make it to Charlottesville that night.

The old WWII veteran, Joel Crofton, put them up for the night then drove them to Charlottesville via the Walton Mountain route.

Since there was no sign of the McGregors, they were about to return home when a balding well dressed man approached. It was Urias.

They thanked Mr. Crofton, then joined Urias walking briskly toward his van.

"Shalom," he greeted them. "When no one came last night we decided to stake out the parking lot."

"No one showed up?" a dismayed Martha said.

"They didn't make it? I wonder if the van broke down." Pastor Don pondered.

"There is no sign of the van this morning. We have had undercover agents looking for it for hours-nothing."

"I bet I know where it will end up- what was it, Shaft 16? If we can get a search warrant. I'll bet they stashed it with..."

"Or have it any of hundreds of other tunnels or already crushed and loaded on a TODT for delivery tonight. I don't think we will find the van."

"How about Tim and Shawnee, what has become of them?"

Now within the safe confines of the van, they were re-introduced to Saul.

"Shalom," he said. "I heard your last question and the best that we can tell you is that they were not in an accident last night but that they did get picked up by a helicopter. An ERWACHE helicopter. If you two had been with them, you would all have been captured."

"At the risk prying, how did you find out what happened to them?"

The agents looked at each other, finally Saul nodding accent.

"ERWACHE has been able to keep it's secrets for so long because it goes to great lengths to know everything about its employees. Every one of their employees is chipped."

"Chipped?"

"You are probably familiar with the practice of chipping dogs for example- should they become lost, then a GPS can track their location."

"GPS being?"

"Global Positioning Satellite. This technology allows people to be tracked to their very location 24/7 and 365. It even works underground or underwater."

"I can't imagine Shawnee willingly letting herself be chipped," Martha declared.

"Our best guess is that when she had to take the company physical they chipped her. It might also have happened when she lost the baby. We intercepted the signal that was coming from Shawnee's..." he paused and then with great hesitation finished, "implant. We know that the implants were either in the forehead or in the hand between the thumb and forefinger. We could pick up the signal for awhile as they flew away, then we lost it."

"Does that mean that they killed Shawnee or ..."

"Cut her hand off? We do not think so. We think they simply deactivated to chip or perhaps are holding the McGregors in a lead lined room somewhere. We don't know if they know we can intercept their chip frequencies or not. We had to have high-level clearance to get this done. The ok had to be sought from Tel Aviv to the top level of your government. We got permission but then the signal was lost."

"Where is all this technology taking us?" Martha asked.

"This stuff came out of the Phoenix project during the Vietnam War." Uri continued, "When your pilots were shot down, at first each carried a radio beacon-kind of a homing device –that rescue aircraft could zero in on. Then rescue could be attempted. Later it became obvious from the nature of some explosions and the short battery life of the transponders, that a better system was needed. So, the CIA began to experiment with implantable chips. Today's chips are for sale on the common market for use as security devices. Each chip is about the size of ¼ of a grain of rice. The chip can be programmed so that an Alzheimer's patient who wanders away can be found."

"Just like a stray dog." Martha mused.

"Precisely. Not only is it possible to encode personal information-name address, phone, social security number, but also bank account information. Think of it- a cashless society, no more need to carry money. No more robberies. No one losing their credit cards. Tracking criminals - a snap. Protect school children from kidnappers. All this is being done to select individuals as we speak."

"Soon coming to a theater near you," Saul added sarcastically.

The Trumbels were sickened by what they heard.

"It's just like John's Revelation. The time will come when you must accept the mark..." Don intoned.

"Or you won't be able to eat or do business," Martha concluded.

"Now you have the better of us-what is John's Revelation?"confessed Rosenberg.

"It's New Testament. A letter written by one of Jesus' disciples describing the end of time and the glory that is heaven. He tells us that only those who accept Jesus will not have to go through the terrible end times. A time of utter chaos and anarchy. Interested in finding out more about Jesus? You know he was a Jew, but His people did not accept Him. I can..."

"Thank you, perhaps later..." Saul said abruptly.

"There may not be a later..."Martha lowly whispered.

In the days that followed, Pastor Don and Martha gathered as much evidence as they could. They were assisted by the ACLJ- the American Center for Law and Justice. Doctor Reynolds tried valiantly to get the FBI and even the United Nations to investigate-but it seemed that no one wanted to check out the story. Unbeknownst to the Trumbels, Uri, Saul, and Dr. Reynolds, -power brokers across several continents were already at work protecting the Krauses. The investigations hoped for, dragged along at a snail's pace.

Without Tim to corroborate Don's testimony, the story quickly was buried and became the stuff upon which tabloids thrive.

" Hillbilly Preacher sees Hitler in Virginia hills!" one of them read.

"Snake charmer hallucinates- Nazis, Nazis everywhere" cried another.

"Sieg Heil in the Hills!" a third read, and then supposed friends of the Trumbels were given free air time on CNN.

"He was one of them fanatics," chastened Robert Davenport, identified as a friend and former member of the Tye River congregation.

"That woman, Mrs.Trumbel, she was so-so churchy, yet she hung with that barmaid, that trashy girl from Lovingston," said another.

"We never knew what to expect from them-they were you know-kinda always reading Scripture to us-I mean this is the 21st century-how important can that stuff be."

The CNN story that night closed with a well groomed reporter tersely stating,

"And that's the latest from the coal fields of Virginia"- in the background, the camera showed the ruined remains of Lobo's Den while final strains of the quaint country song *Long Black Veil* wafted across the television screens of millions nationwide.

Far away, media moguls were smiling as once again they had circled the wagons and protected one of their own from investigation.

The Krauses were never found and the evidence that Don and Tim had seen was destroyed by a series of mine cave-ins, triggered by skillfully planted doses of dynamite. Evidence of human cruelty, unequalled since the Holocaust, were entombed beneath Virginia's soil.

Network news coverage concluded with the Soros funded watch words of the day, some variation of - "Just look at all that the Krauses had done for the poor and underprivileged of Virginia."

CBS closed with, "Despite the unsubstantiated charges, the Krauses employed the poor and downtrodden."

ABC-"It was the hallmark of the ERWACHE Corporation to help the poor..."

NBC-"Poor people and especially the handicapped were hired here..."

ESPN- "Don Trumbel wouldn't be the first football player to have taken one too many shots to the head. He probably did not realize all the good that ERWACHE was doing for the mountain people. He wasn't a native Virginian."

MSNBC –"Whatever may be said, the Krauses looked out for the poor. Perhaps no other corporation in America had a greater interest in poor people than ERWACHE."

Indeed.

Chapter 32

"We should have been able to piece together the clues," Martha lamented.

"How so Mrs. Trumbel?" asked FBI agent Nolan. "You reported what you knew as soon as you could verify it."

"Still we just should have known."

"We all missed it. The hog renderings, the kidnapping of children, the evil of those people," added Pastor Trumbel.

"Money drives people to commit heinous acts," stated Agent Torgelson.

"The Love of money is ..." Don's voice trailed off.

"What was it about Shawnee that the Krauses hated?" Nolan asked

"She was not one of their puppets-she had a free will and she was a Christian. She was the antithesis of everything that ERWACHE stood for," Martha responded.

"So where does the investigation stand?" Don asked.

"Dead in the water. We believe that you uncovered a world-wide conspiracy that deals with buying time."

"Buying time? How?"

Torgelson continued, "Dr.Krause was/is a specialist in aging. Apparently, ERWACHE has been marketing human baby stem cells to rich clients throughout the world. It seems that rich people will pay tens of thousands of dollars for one injection. The promise is eternal youth."

"Eternal life- can only happen through one man and it isn't Josef Mengele Krause," Martha affirmed.

"ERWACHE was offering the fountain of youth at the expense of the most innocent among us-the pre-born child." Agent Benton contributed. "Those TODTs were filled with aborted children and kidnapped children from across the USA. We have tracked some TODTs but the connections are inconclusive."

"So down in that hell hole- under the auto shop," Don began.

"Was a human chop shop where babies were stripped of the desired cells, the remains either fed to the pigs or dumped in the ocean or both." Agent Nolan said. "Others who possessed the correct genes were either raped or sterilized to create what ERWACHE had for sale."

"So some people were drugged and then enslaved?" Torgelson speculated, "Possibly, or possibly lobotomized-kept alive until no longer of use then..."

"That would make perfect sense!" Martha said interrupting."I remember Shawnee seeing a girl she had met appearing zombie-like."

"And that would explain why those we saw in cages responding to light but not to our voices." Don added.

"It also explains why those being raped did not resist."

"So what happens now? Probably no church in America will touch me, although Professor Reynolds has promised me that he will..."Don began."

"Professor Reynolds has been reported missing by his wife," interrupted Agent Nolan.

The reality that this was no game once again hit them.

"We'd like you to go underground-in conjunction with the Israelis, until we can trace the Krauses. They are much too egocentric to stay out of sight for long."

"We don't know for how long you would stay out of sight but perhaps you could aid the Israelis. They always need extra hands."

"In truth, what do you think? Will we ever see the McGregors again?" asked Martha.

 "We hope so," confirmed Agent Nolan.

"You and I will, if not here, then when we are called home," Don stated.

"Here are your new identities." Torgelson offered.

"We know who are through Jesus Christ. We have been told that much of what ERWACHE did was in plain view. We will try to help, but we go without new identities. We have a friend who will never leave us or forsake us. Thanks anyway."

Breinigsville, PA USA
23 November 2009
228078BV00001B/1/P